ANYWHERE
BUT
BORDEAUX!

ANYWHERE BUT BORDEAUX!

ADVENTURES OF AN AMERICAN TEACHER IN FRANCE

JACQUELINE KING DONNELLY

Editor Judyth Hill: Cover and book design Mary Meade. *Anywhere but Bordeaux!* is available on Amazon.com.

Cover photograph of the author by Gale Beery

All photographs in *Anywhere but Bordeaux!* by Jacqueline King Donnelly
unless otherwise credited.

Jacqueline King Donnelly —1st ed.
978-1713214403

I would like to dedicate this book to my dear husband and best friend, Patrick, who lived this adventure with me, supporting me in every way through the highs and lows of our year in France, and patiently proofread multiple versions of this story

And to my darling children, who with their families, are the joy of our lives.

Disclaimer

In this memoir, I have recreated events, locales and conversations from my memories of them. All of the events in this memoir are true to the best of my recollection.

In order to maintain anonymity and respect privacy, in most instances I have changed the names of individuals and places. I also may have changed some identifying characteristics and details such as physical properties, occupations and places of residence to further assure their privacy.

The opinions expressed in this memoir are solely those of the author.

"Twenty years from now you will be more disappointed by the things that you didn't do than by the ones you did do. So throw off the bowlines. Sail away from the safe harbor. Catch the trade winds in your sails. Explore. Dream. Discover."

—Mark Twain

Contents

September

October

November

December

January

February

March

April

May

June

Preface
WHAT I'D LIKE YOU TO KNOW

THE OLDER WE GET, the quicker the days seem to flow;
seasons pass, and the years fly by. It happens so fast, that looking
back in time, our lives can seem like a blur.

And yet, through it all, we remember certain key experiences
that stand out above the rest.

These events are so significant they form our very being.

Perhaps it is a casual remark we heard as a child which in-
spired us, a disaster we thankfully averted, a success we savored,
or a loss so painful it takes years to heal.

These memories are so vivid, so profound, we are compelled
to tell and re-tell them, and in so doing, peel them away from
our souls.

You are about to read my story of a year unlike any other.

It is the year I taught English in a middle school in the Bordeaux region of France.

It has marked me for life.

Am I the heroine of the story?

It is for you to judge, since I weathered the year sometimes
well, sometimes not.

This is the story I must tell, and I want to share it with you.

Prologue
WHY I JUMPED SHIP

HAVE YOU EVER WANTED to run away? I mean, leave everything behind — your home, your work, your friends?

Have you ever thought, *I really have to get out of here, this is just not working for me anymore...?*

You feel so entrenched in your life, you long for an escape hatch?

I felt that primal urge to run, and I did... and this is my story.

My life is close to perfect. Happily married, two well-adjusted cats, family and friends nearby, and unlike when we were newlyweds, we can now easily pay our bills.

But suddenly it was not enough.

I have been teaching French in a high school for over 25 years. Although I love the magic of interacting with my students and seeing them progress in the language, the monotony of the school year is deadening.

There is a predictable pattern of highs and lows repeated the same way year after year.

This is what I mean:

August is a time of euphoria. Working in the classroom to get the bulletin boards ready, counting the textbooks and workbooks, smelling the sweet smell of late summer wafting through the windows. This is a time of optimism and energy, of determination that this year my teaching will be even better than the last.

This high continues into late September and October, as the students settle into course work, still tan from summer fun, sporting new clothes and fresh attitudes. The fall season is peppered with football games and rallies. Oh yes, school is a lot of fun.

Dreary November drains enthusiasm as withering leaves drop from the trees with endless days of pouty grey clouds and rain.

Then the first cold, sniffles, and coughs, and it is downhill from then on until the sugar high days before Christmas when the students exchange gifts and prepare for the holidays.

January, colorless, and cold: exam preparation and testing, with the unrelentingly dull weather of winter, brightened just a bit by the red valentines exchanged among friends in February.

March and April, teachers and students white-knuckle it until spring vacation, which always seems to be yet another week away.

May brings warm weather and awakens latent frisky energy in the students, making teaching almost impossible.

And then, June. Ah, June. Exams, grades, locking the classroom. Driving away from school for the last time until August feels intoxicating.

And so it goes, year after year after year after year...

The conversation in the teachers' lounge devolves from what exciting approaches they are experimenting with, to the hot topic of how many days each teacher has until retirement.

Even seasoned, dedicated educators can feel like prisoners. "Hey, how long are you in for?"

"Are you going to take the early retirement package or stick it out for a few more years?"

The most tedious part of the school day is lunchtime in the lounge.

Virginia eats the same cheese sandwich, pickle, and apple from the same wrinkled recycled paper bag.

Henry always talks with his mouth full of egg salad; Myra just can't quite finish the half bowl of tomato soup she warms up in the microwave, and Tom always slices his apple in half, then fourths, then eighths.

It all is so predictable.

Every day, I look around the lounge and think, there has to be more than to life than this.

It is at this point that I, on the brink of retirement with a couple of years left, want to jump ship.

I gotta get out of here. I have to try something new.

Then the phone call.

My colleague, Patricia, rings to ask if I know of someone who has an apartment to rent for her exchange teacher.

What exchange teacher?

Patricia has found a crack in the wall.

She has been accepted by an international exchange program to teach in an elementary school in England for a year. Patricia will work in the British school, and her counterpart will teach Patricia's classes in her school.

Ah, this gets my criminal mind working.

I could go teach in France!

Having taught for more than two decades, I have gotten pretty good at it.

I love my students.

I love my home.

Yet there is something madcap, wild and reckless in us all that could tempt us to dream of chucking it all for adventure.

The one thing I know for sure, based on the description in the French textbooks, is that French schools, unlike ours, have serious students who do their work. Discipline problems? Not in a French school.

Teaching there will be a piece of cake.

And should there be any adjustment problems, being a seasoned teacher, I will overcome them. No worries there.

I was born to teach French.

My parents indulged me when I was seven by setting up a class-room in the basement of our home with a bulletin board, black-board, desk, and two student desks they found somewhere. My three favorite dolls were my first students. Every day I taught them what I learned in first grade.

After two dreadful years of Latin in high school, I elected to take French.

From the first day in class, when I heard the music of the language, I fell madly in love with it.

I could not learn French quickly enough. My parents hired French tutors who worked with me after school to accelerate my learning, and I elected to forgo the beach to do summer study. Eventually, I majored in French in college and graduate school, before embarking on a long career teaching the language I dearly love.

My passion for French and the French people has never waned.

So, every fiber in me is ready for this Gallic adventure, the capstone of a life of passionate learning and teaching.

I lose myself in dreams of being in France, sipping espresso in a café, walking hand in hand with my husband along the Seine, munching on a baguette we bought at our favorite bakery, and above all, speaking French.

Putting my devious plan into motion is the next step.

There will be a few hurdles to jump, but my heart is calling me to do this.

I look at Same Sandwich Virginia, Egg Salad Henry, Half Soup Myra, and Apple Slicer Tom and hum to myself, "You're going to miss me when I'm gone."

April

CHAPTER 1

How it All Began

THE DESIRE TO LEAVE the certain, the sure, the safety of my well-measured life is so compelling it cannot be denied. I wait for the best time to broach the subject to my sweet, unsuspecting husband, Patrick.

Nestled on a settee on the screened-in porch overlooking our little lake, sipping the last of the bottle of Sauvignon Blanc, I let the idea slip out of my mouth and into a reality that will take us far away from our idyllic little nest in the woods.

"Patrick, let's live in France."

Patrick's gaze turns from the heron soaring over the water. "Where did this idea of France come from?" Patrick is no stranger to my schemes; in fact, he has come to trust my intuition about when we need change in our lives.

"I think it will be fun for us," I continue. "I always wanted to teach a year in France before I retire, the kids are gone, and we can get my sister to take the cats."

We are finally at that time in our lives when we can soon retire; we have no strings, and we are both feeling that live-it-up-before-we-die nudge.

When I was 26, I met Patrick, a tall wild-haired Irishman, during a summer I was spending at our family cottage in Michigan, where I had exiled myself from my precious Boston to cram for my French master's examinations, which were scheduled for mid-August.

Since I was spending six hours a day studying and had little distractions at the cottage other than rereading the French classics, I decided to go out with him.

I don't know if it was the charm of his unruly black hair, with a shock of impertinent grey at his temples, or the kindness in his heart he so carefully tried to hide beneath a tough guy composure, but I deeply and irrevocably fell in love with him - which was not at all on my schedule for the summer.

I had dated many men but never felt the passion I felt for him.

And the sentiment was returned.

Soon I was to return to Boston for my exams. The impending separation weighed on us both, but we didn't speak of it directly.

I waited for the magic words that seemed to be stuck in his heart.

I finally asked, "Patrick, when are you going to tell me you love me?" He looked at me tenderly and blurted out, "Oh, Jackie, I love you."

A few days later, after this prompted declaration, we planned to go out on a date.

Before his arrival, I walked from the cottage to the bluff overlooking Lake Michigan, a short distance away. Although early in the evening, the sky was stone grey, two massive weather fronts were swirling, blending, separating, seemingly in combat overhead, threatening a violent storm. I was filled with the presence of God. I prayed, "Dear God, I love him so much. If he is the one, please give me a sign."

I returned to the cottage.

He arrived at the house.

After a perfunctory greeting to my parents, he suggested we go look at the lake. At the very spot where I had prayed, he took me in his arms and said: "Jackie, I do not have the right to ask you this since we have dated such a short time, but will you marry me?"

Without a pause, I replied, "Patrick, I am going to have to spend time thinking this over, but right now, I am afraid the answer is yes."

Joy!

The next morning, after the storm, the lake was placid, hidden in a deep fog. Patrick was becalmed in a sailing race, wondering what he had done; at the same time, I was looking out the window of our cottage at the cottony low clouds hovering over the water, wondering the same.

Despite these post-engagement doubts, we have traveled life's path together for 47 years, raising two children, Mark and Beth, each married, living away but close to our hearts.

With time, my Patrick's wild, black hair has faded to grey, his taut stomach is less than washboard, but his blue eyes and kind heart are only more intense.

We have never feared to follow our instincts or to do daring things. Well into my career, I took a leave from my French teaching post in our local high school to give a month-long seminar in Grenoble, teaching at a French university while Patrick worked that month in Japan.

In Grenoble, I lived in a French host home in the shadow of the Alps. I was Madame Donnelly, *le Professeur*. It was so stimulating and exotic that this brief sojourn whetted my appetite for a longer adventure.

Patrick stands up, stretches, and walks into the kitchen, returning with another bottle of wine and a calendar.

"How will we work this out?" he asks.

"I think the first step is to float it past Susan, my principal, to see if she is willing to let me leave as well as take on a French faculty member in exchange. I can get the application online, and we can go from there."

Patrick, who is on the fence about the timing of his retirement, begins to muse aloud about pulling the ripcord and terminating his career.

In France, he can assume the new role of househusband, meal planner, and trip coordinator for a year while I teach. From time to time during the year, he will have to return to the States for business board meetings, but that is feasible.

There is a long silence as he turns his wine glass in his hand. "Let's go for it! What have we got to lose?"

With a clink of our glasses and a flurry of musings about the romance of living in France, we talk for hours about what we will have to do to pull up anchor and leave.

CHAPTER 2

Activating the Plan

THE NEXT DAY I leave for work early, giving myself enough time to talk to Susan, who is my friend as well as my administrator, before morning classes.

I greet the secretary and walk into Susan's office, where her face is hidden behind a large screen computer. She looks up and smiles.

"How's it going? What's new?"

"Susan, I have an idea." I sit down and lay out my carefully rehearsed proposition.

She listens intently as I unfold the plan, covering every aspect of the mechanics of the international teacher exchange. The program is prestigious and can offer a positive benefit to the school.

My French program has grown over the years to five full classes. This exchange could only be a bonus to the students.

Susan agrees to support me.

"I think this is a great idea. We will need to get the superintendent on board, but I don't see a problem with it."

The application is straightforward: "Why do you want to be an exchange teacher; what can you bring to the program, and what skills do you possess that will make you successful?"

Over the next week, I write and rewrite a strong essay outlining my teaching background; 25 years as a high school and college

French teacher, creator of innovative language programs, fluent in French, and possessing a deep understanding of the French people and culture. I throw everything possible into the mix, so I will be accepted, and we can go to France.

In the application, I have to indicate if I want to teach high school or am open to teaching middle school as well.

I have never taught middle school, but think: How hard can this be?

I include the middle school option to increase my chances of teaching in France.

Patrick and I receive a letter indicating we will be interviewed at a small suburban college outside of Chicago. We set out on the three-hour trip with a carefully assembled dossier of the required documents.

The university is foreboding: a cluster of stern Victorian brick buildings each with tall rectangular windows set in frames of stone, with faded, honey-colored double wooden doors, giving the overall impression of a mental sanitarium.

We climb polished linoleum stairs to the third floor of building C, following the paper arrows, "Teacher Exchange Interviews." On the large bulletin board at the landing are posted notices of future lectures, dances, and requests for rides tacked willy-nilly in any available space.

We sit on metal folding chairs in the hallway outside classroom 306 flanked by other candidates. At first, we all eye each other like prisoners on death row. Who will be accepted, and who will not? Soon, everyone breaks into light conversation.

"Where are you hoping to teach?"

Some are applying to Spain, another couple, with children, to Germany. We relax when we realize no direct competitors are vying for France.

Patrick and I decide we will answer the questions cautiously, not offering any information that might work against us.

When we hear "Mr. and Mrs. Donnelly," we follow a kindly looking woman, the majordomo, to the committee room.

Before us, seated at a large wooden table, are three interviewers, their hands resting on stacks of files. The senior member, a grey-haired woman with glasses too big for her face, finds our application and begins the inquisition.

We answer the questions posed in the application tersely but with measured enthusiasm, like orphans interviewing for an adoption.

"Of course, you realize even if your credentials are in order, you may not be chosen to serve as an exchange teacher if there is not a good fit for you and your French counterpart." she cautions.

This ominous warning dims our hopes we will be accepted.

"You will receive an envelope in shortly with your exchange information or a letter thanking you for your participation in the selection process."

With that, we drive home, debating what our chances will be.

Patrick and I love France. We have traveled there at least 35 times, so we know every corner of the hexagon very well, as the French refer to their country. The only city we never warmed to is Bordeaux.

The first time we visited Bordeaux, it was during the Tour de France and the competitors were biking through the outskirts of the city. Because of this world-class event, we were detoured through unsavory parts of town. The combination of fatigue and annoyance added to the aversion we had to the city.

Also, Bordeaux, at the time, lacked the charm of Paris.

The large medieval tower at the entrance to the city seemed menacing.

The exterior of the buildings appeared dirty grey, not the polished white facades of the capital. There were no elegant Haussmann black wrought iron balustrades on the buildings we were used to seeing in Paris.

In short, the city of Bordeaux seemed to us to be tired and worn, and of all the cities in France we have visited, Bordeaux was our least favorite.

From a gut level, we simply didn't like it.

When the thick package arrives in April, we are delighted it is heavily laden with documents. "The Exchange would not write us a Dear John letter with so much stuff, right?" I ask.

"Who is going to open it?"

We flip a coin to add to the drama.

I win.

"Oh, my gosh, Patrick, could this really be it?

Where are we going to go?"

Before I break the seal, I ask Patrick what his wish would be.

Without hesitation, he replies, "Anywhere but Bordeaux."

Indeed, from the welcome letter, we learn we are accepted into the program, but the information about our exchange partner will not be revealed until this mystery person accepts the offer as well.

This is too much torture!

We divine the postal code for the unknown area: 33. I run to my Michelin guide to France and search where that can be.

It is Bordeaux!

"Oh well. Hey, it has to have gotten better since when we were there. Just think of the wine we will drink!" Patrick reasons.

The next step, of course, is to learn where in Bordeaux we are going, who the exchange teacher is, and where I will be teaching.

A week later, I receive word the exchange teacher has accepted the position in our school.

We learn Monique Aubin is a middle school teacher of English. Her husband, Jean, and two teenage children, Jennifer and Roger, will live in the States with her during the school year. They live outside of Bordeaux in a little rural community called St. Pierre in the heart of the wine country.

My assignment is to teach English to 6th, 7th, and 8th graders while she will be teaching French I, II, and III to my freshmen through senior students. Both of us have taken the dare to teach outside of our fields of study since I am not a middle school English teacher, and she has never taught French at the secondary level.

No problem. We both are willing to take on the challenge.

Patrick and I start to imagine a small country home where we will wander through rows of grapes, picking a few along to the way to taste and enjoy. We will make friends with our neighbors, travel a lot in France on the weekends, and love our new French life.

This is going to work out just fine!

CHAPTER 3

The Plot Thickens

THE EXCHANGE HAS PROVIDED Monique's contact information.

I call her from school to break the ice, introducing myself, and explaining a bit about the job she will be taking on.

"*Bonjour,*" I say, and continue in French, "What a wonderfully exciting adventure is before us!"

Monique is a bit more cautious. Asking me a lot of questions, she appears not quite committed to the project. This makes my stomach knot.

Since Monique will soon be on vacation, she announces she and her family will travel from France to see the school and community firsthand.

We are delighted to have the opportunity to meet them. Hopefully, after visiting our school and community, she will be fully committed to the exchange.

When they pull in the driveway on a brisk April day, we go out to meet them with open arms. We have corresponded so much we feel we already know them.

Monique is a tall, slim, fiftyish woman with mid-length straight blond hair and a measured smile, who gives me the quick French peck on each cheek as a greeting. As she enters our house, her eyes dart from side to side, quickly assessing our house.

Her husband Jean is shorter than she, stocky, buzz-cut hair, deep blue eyes. He seems relaxed and peaceful within himself and used to trailing behind his wife as she is clearly the leader of the pack.

Their daughter, Jennifer, is slim and trendy, her long hair casually thrown into a messy knot. She wears an American logo sweatshirt over her T-shirt and jeans.

Roger, their son, like many teenagers, is shy. He lags behind, almost reluctant to enter the house as this is an out-of-France experience and probably unsettling.

In our communications before her arrival, Monique and I weigh whether or not we will exchange houses or find lodging for each other. The question is still unresolved at this point, although she has already offered her home as an option.

We live in a contemporary house we designed with all windows oriented to our "Golden Pond" lake, which is dazzling under the crisp spring sun.

To others, our little lake might look more like a large pond surrounded on three sides by woods and a dotting of four houses. The road on the far side of the water cuts a path through more woods. The wind is always variable and creates wispy crosshatch patterns on the lake according to the caprice of the breeze.

Our large lawn extends to a dock where lounge chairs beckon, inviting one to enjoy many lazy afternoons.

We show them the master bedroom. It is spacious, with a fireplace and a small private balcony. Monique comments that bedrooms in France are never that large.

The kitchen-dining room area is open concept, with a small half wall separating the two sections. Jean loves the large skylights, which allow the house to be bathed in natural sunlight and give one the impression of almost being outdoors.

At this point, our visitors think this is simply a home tour.

As they are admiring the view of the lake from the windows, we proudly announce we want them to stay here.

"Welcome home. This will be your house now."

Monique turns and says, "I feel guilty and uncomfortable. Our house is not as nice as yours."

I counter, "Monique, that is not important. We want to live like the French in France; we don't have to have the same kind of home to make this successful." Although I reassure her, it makes me wonder what her house is like.

The kids are delighted and stake out their bedrooms, which are on the lower level.

Her husband, Jean, who will leave his business for a year and become a househusband like Patrick, is fascinated by the kitchen, the spice drawer, the cooktop, and announces this year he is going to become a chef.

Leaving the family to visit with Patrick, I drive Monique to the school to show her my large classroom, the computer area, CD/DVD player, and projection screen.

The French textbooks are a state-of-the-art series with audio and video supplements which work to bring France into the classroom. Monique is pleased to see the teacher's guides, which will give her step-by-step hints as to how to plan her lessons.

Monique paws through the books on the counter, walks around the classroom touching models of *La Tour Eiffel* and the *Arc de Triomphe* the students have created, before turning to me saying, "I feel guilty doing this exchange because my school is not as nice and it has problems."

I dismiss this ominous remark.

"Oh, Monique, I am sure I will be fine. Isn't this exciting?"

The next day, Monique will be introduced to Susan, the faculty, and my students, who are more than anxious to meet their future teacher.

That evening Patrick and Jean conspire to plan what our first meal together will entail. In an international collaboration, the men sip wine and grill steaks for the family's first American meal in their new home. Jennifer and Roger set out to explore the walking trails in the woods after dinner while the four of us do the dishes together.

CHAPTER 4

Hesitation Waltz

SOMETIMES WE JUST KNOW something to be true. It is a glimmer inside us, an inkling that just won't go away. We silence it at our peril, for it is so often an infallible road marker of what might be.

The next day Monique and I have an early breakfast at the dining table overlooking the lake. The sky, still pink and mauve from sunrise, is reflected in the glassy water.

We leave early for school so Monique can meet Susan, her future colleagues, and, most importantly, my students.

Monique does not fail to look chic: slender in a grey pencil skirt, a black blouse with discreet silver buttons, high heels, and the de rigueur scarf tied nonchalantly about her neck, as only French women know how to do.

I am very proud to show her off; because she looks so French, she will meet everyone's expectations.

After a perfunctory meet and greet with the administration and secretaries, Monique accompanies me to attend my classes.

The students are wide-eyed, cautious, if not fearful. I introduce her to them, reminding them how fortunate they will be next year to have a real live French teacher.

We live in a small town. Most students have never met a French person, yet they are studying the language. This will be a wonderful opportunity for them to have authentic contact.

Monique then speaks to them in French, much too quickly for their comprehension. The students stir and laugh nervously.

"Who knows what Madame said?" I ask, jumping in to break the tension.

Silence.

"Monique, would you repeat what you said, more slowly this time?" Slowing down her rapid-fire speech, she introduces herself again, excessively drawing out each word. She cannot maintain that slow pace for long and unconsciously returns to her fast cadence.

This scene repeats itself four more times as she meets my other classes.

As she speaks, my eyes pan the room. Something about her, not the speed of her speech, but the cool, lack of affect toward the students disturbs me. It is as if she broadcasts but cannot read the students' eyes to know they are not following.

I feel like a parent who, at the last minute, doubts the skill and care of the babysitter I have just hired.

Inside me, deep down, beyond my control, is that voice saying clearly, "This is a mistake. This woman is not going to nurture your students the way you do." The image of lambs to slaughter is inescapable.

Is it too late to pull out? Will I look foolish if I change my mind?
I can't pull out now. It's not fair to Monique.
Don't I have the right to pursue my dream?
She will be fine. She will be fine. She will be fine.

But I fear she will not, and the students will pay the price.

We meet my colleagues for lunch. Monique listens to our banter with a thin, tense smile, engaging appropriately.

She is asked how she likes the school.

"It is so much bigger than my school, and you have so many

things here. We in France accomplish things with much less, but we succeed very well. It is impressive but not necessary."

Thud.

Patrick drives her children to school in the afternoon to register for classes. Jennifer is streetwise beyond her years. She has watched American television in France and expects an authentic *Happy Days* experience.

Meeting a few students in the hall, she plays the French girl to the hilt. This year is going to be her game.

Monique oversees the enrollment. "We are here this year so our children can learn English." This remark confirms my fears she is less than invested in teaching my students for whom I have great affection.

Roger is shy. He follows behind us to the counselor's office to register for classes.

Jennifer is offered the senior menu of challenging classes, which she declines. "I don't want to work that hard this year." Instead, she opts for the general education classes taken by C or D average students designed to get them through.

Roger accepts what is offered to him without question. His love is track. As long as he can participate on a team, he knows he will love the school year.

Jean sees an opportunity for connecting not only with his son but with the community. He volunteers to work with the track team.

That night, as we lay in bed, I whisper to Patrick that I fear I am making a great mistake leaving my students to her. There is just something....

Patrick soothes me, saying, "You can't be sure. Give her a chance. The students will be fine."

But I know. I know...

CHAPTER 5

Hesitation Waltz...
And the Beat Goes On

THE NEXT DAY MONIQUE and I sit at the dining room table, planning an exchange of pen pal letters and videos between our two schools, hoping to bring together the French and American students.

My students know French kids from their language textbooks, where they are portrayed as perfect little teenagers willing to go to the movies only after they have studied for hours in the library. They are caricatures of young people who are neither appealing nor realistic.

Why learn a language if the kids are such geeks? my students reason.

Monique and I hope by filming students from each school in their daily life, as they really are, they will feel motivated to learn to communicate with each other. It is an idealistic goal, an effort of global understanding on a minor level.

Since Patrick will return monthly to the States, he will be the go-between, ferrying materials back and forth.

We are optimistic but naïve, thinking this will work since, at that time, there was no Skype, Facetime, Facebook, or other social media. The time difference between France and the United States makes communication in real time impossible. Yet still, we are willing to try.

This exchange allays my guilt to a certain extent, believing my students and I will still be in touch.

Monique mentions more than once that our American school seems well organized. She feels uneasy because the students at her school are, as she puts it, *naughty.*

I dismiss this remark as just conversation. Surely her school cannot be that bad.

Monique and her family leave for France, assured the school, the community, and the house will satisfy them.

We say an affectionate goodbye, all of us hopeful this exchange is going to be a success.

Returning to school after her visit, I want to judge the reactions of the students. Each class needs reassurance Monique will be a good teacher.

"You will get used to the way she speaks. She really wants to teach you and see you succeed."

And I really want to believe this.

After one particular class ends, as the students are filing out, a young Hispanic girl lingers behind to talk to me.

"Madame, I don't want you to go. For the first time, because of you, I like school. I love the way you teach. And I love your class: I feel very safe in it."

Her name is Ana. Ana is very intelligent but shy. She is short, with large brown eyes, a timid smile, long black ponytail, always dressed in jeans and a T-shirt.

Her family entered the United States illegally, dodging bullets as they crossed the border. She works at a pizza restaurant after school to help support her family.

I am half-listening to her as I shuffle papers on my desk and cram test papers into my briefcase.

I stop.

Ana embodies every fear and doubt I have about the exchange and personifies the personal price some students might pay for my absence.

"Ana, you will be fine. And we can email each other to stay in touch. You are special to me too."

We do not speak of this again. We do not have to: everything has been said.

As the school year winds down, I devote more time to organizing lesson plans and setting out materials for Monique to use to make her teaching easier.

It is how one prepares a dinner party: setting the table in anticipation of giving your guests the best possible experience.

Each class wishes me well at the end of the school year with cards, little gifts, and hugs.

I turn the key and leave my school as I hum my favorite song, "I Will Survive." This is really going to happen!

June

CHAPTER 6

Reconnaissance Mission: Scoping Out Bordeaux

ACCEPTING MONIQUE'S INVITATION TO visit, I fly to Paris shortly after the end of school.

Joëlle, my Parisian friend, picks me up at Charles de Gaulle Airport, a ritual repeated annually for over 20 years. She manages to wedge my suitcase into her small VW, and off we go to her apartment in the 12th arrondissement, a district on the east edge of Paris. It still untouched by the double-decker tourist buses traveling up and down the *Champs-Élysées.*

Joëlle is a divorcee who still has a working relationship with her husband since they share a daughter who now lives independently in an apartment in Paris. Joëlle is a physician specializing in medical research for the pharmaceutical industry.

We take the small elevator up to the fifth floor. Her living room is tastefully laid out. On the left, two stiff, formal chairs sit symmetrically side by side. Against the wall, a coffee brown leather sofa with a cushion at either end, a glass cocktail table with stacked art books, a small two-shelf étagère displaying bar glasses, and as a focal point, a large abstract painting which even today I do not understand.

I settle in her small tidy office, which converts to a bedroom by opening a futon. I put my computer on her desk next to carefully cut white computer paper attached to a clip which she recycles for a notepad.

She is very sentimental. Her bookshelves not only house novels neatly arranged by height, but years of photo albums recording travels, summer sojourns, and family celebrations. She is meticulously neat since her apartment is so small. That is also her scientific nature. Her apartment reminds me of a sailboat where every niche is carefully laid out to maximize space.

Joëlle is so tolerant of my excess. Her office quickly looks more like a clothing store by the time I unpack.

Joëlle and I have spent many hours over dinner and red wine, discussing what makes Americans and the French see the world differently. Even though I speak the language, have studied their great thinkers through the ages, and have lived among them, I still don't understand the French. Joëlle, who seems so reasonable to my American eyes, will often react so differently to a situation than I would. She, like her compatriots, is far more skeptical about life than I am, more tenuous about showing enthusiasm and more cautious about people.

Joëlle is very curious about Monique and her family, posing many questions to which, as yet, I have no answers. She can't wait until I return from Bordeaux so she can debrief me about my future life in France.

Joëlle is like a mother hen. At the end of our visit, she accompanies me to the Montparnasse train station, helps me buy my ticket, and teaches me how to validate it before I board. When she is satisfied I have the wherewithal to survive, she gives me a quick peck on each cheek and leaves for work.

Boarding the train, I am disappointed to see I am not alone in a standard seat.

Instead, my assigned place is near the window directly across from a French couple. We are separated only by a rectangular table. It is our fate to face each other for the whole three-hour transit.

The train rumbles slowly out of the station, gently jostling us, passing the outlying industrial areas, grey public housing units, small suburban areas punctuated by train stations and parking lots, until we reach the countryside where the train picks up speed. With a good stare and a lot of patience, I can make out the cathedral of Chartres in the distance, which looks like a schooner sailing through fields of hay.

This area called *la Beauce,* or "breadbasket" looks like a Millet painting: a sweet, gentle landscape of farmhouses, geometric fields of grain, and little villages.

We stop at appointed stations where travelers gather their bags, newspaper and coats before descending the train to go to their homes or await a friend's pick-up.

I had bought a sandwich, chips, and a coke from a vendor under the large clock in the station before boarding but feel awkward taking it out and putting it on our shared table, so I wait.

Immediately at noon, as if a bell has rung, the people in our compartment extract their lunches which they purchased or packed. In my little family group, I see sandwiches, fruit, cheese, and sparkling water.

I, in turn, take out my meal and offer a weak *Bon appétit* to the family before beginning to eat.

This gesture breaks the ice. Curious about their traveling companion, they begin to ask me questions: where am I going, how long will I be in France, have I ever been to Bordeaux?

Since that is their destination, I decide not to share how much I really do not like their city but speak in general platitudes about my love of France, which indeed is sincere.

An hour before our arrival, the scenery turns from rolling wheat fields to vineyards, which whet my appetite for discovering my new home. This is really where we are going to live!

As we pull into the St. Jean train station, I leave my traveling companions, who wish me *bon courage*, and descend the train like a waif looking for her parents.

Monique and Jean, Jennifer and Roger weave their way through the oncoming throng of travelers on the quay and greet me warmly. I embrace each one, heads bobbing from side to side as we kiss each cheek.

We pile in their small car and set out for Saint Pierre. The trip takes 30 minutes on a four-lane highway past the *Maison des Vins de Bordeaux*, a commercial tasting center I mentally put on my list of places to visit. I am a bit disappointed we are going to live so far from the city center.

We exit the highway and follow a tar road through two villages before arriving at our destination.

Jean slows the car down in front of a double-gated entry to their parking area. He opens the garage doors with an electric control.

The massive gates open slowly like gates to a castle keep.

"Now, don't expect much," Monique cautions. "It isn't grand, you know."

My first impression is of a *mas* or house in the south of France that typically has a clay tile roof, creamy stucco walls, and mahogany-colored shutters.

Shutters always fascinated me as a child. In fairy tales, they may open to allow the beautiful damsel in the tower to let down her long billowing hair to escape the witch who has imprisoned her - or - be locked tight to enclose nasty ogres in their lairs.

But these shutters are innocent enough.

The first-floor windows facing a small swimming pool have vertical bars on them. I have never been in a home with bars, and it gives me the impression of being in jail.

The house is indeed small but will be perfect for the two of us.

We enter through the garage into a small utility room where Monique drops her purse on her desk. This is her spot. Years of art books, decorating magazines, and English novels are stacked on aluminum shelving.

Upon entry into the house proper, I see an old computer and printer which fit tightly into a corner nook.

The living area is to the right, with an oblong walnut dining table flanked by ladderback chairs. An artificial flower arrangement in a round vase is in the center of the table; her Bavarian pink and purple flower plates are displayed in a breakfront against the wall.

Nearby, against the opposite wall, a television, VCR, and 5 disk CD player form a modest entertainment unit. A large toffee-colored leather couch and love seat placed in an L-arrangement allow for formal entertaining or casual relaxation near the fireplace.

The multiple remote controls are on the low coffee table.

The kitchen is in the back of the house. The single sink, small stove, and refrigerator line the walls. The washer/dryer unit is under the counter area near the sink.

Since the weather is warm, the door to the veranda and the garden is open, giving a sense of space and nature.

There are two dark bedrooms on the main floor. Across from them is a small bathroom with a tub and shower. The tiles on the wall are a faint lavender with drooping lilies.

The WC is separate and can be seen at the end of the hall.

A narrow nautical-type staircase leads to the master bedroom in a loft above the living room.

I *oooh* and *aaah* appropriately as I am shown about, thinking this will indeed be a nice home for us. The excitement of the moment prevents me from looking at the house critically.

I settle in my room by putting a few outfits in the large carved wooden armoire. Opening it, I smell old wood, must, and varnish.

I rejoin the family on the little terrace, where we sip an aperitif and nibble on mixed nuts and olives.

We go into Bordeaux for dinner at an outdoor restaurant, one among ten, set up outdoors in a large square, *la Place du Parlement*.

The white-jacketed waiters with perky black bow ties and long white aprons extending to their pant cuffs scurry, carrying trays of drinks or plates of food.

The summer breeze, the setting sun which gilds the columns of the buildings, and a repast with my new colleague and her family create a perfect moment; all of Bordeaux is flirting with me, and I am so susceptible.

Returning home, Monique announces it is time for bed.

Retiring to my room, I look out through the shutters to the pool and the vineyards beyond the curving road, appreciating the evening breeze and trying to decompress and take pleasure in the moment.

Monique flies in the room, passes before me, and closes the shutters sliding the heavy bolt. "We never sleep with the windows open, always shuttered," she announces, leaving no room for protest.

The room has no fresh air, and I feel like I am suffocating. For hours I toss restlessly, my mind racing with jumbled scenes from the day, fears, and a haunting worry I am over my head and out of my mind for taking this adventure on.

CHAPTER 7

First Impressions

TODAY, MONIQUE PLANS TO take me to school. As her first class is at 11, we have a leisurely breakfast in the garden eating the croissants Jean brought back from the bakery and enjoying a healthy cup of *café au lait*.

Monique grabs her keys, and as an afterthought, puts a bottle of red wine in her attaché case to share with the faculty at lunch to celebrate my visit to the school.

I look forward to this opportunity of meeting my new colleagues and appreciate this festive gesture.

I attend her class sitting in the back of the room, which gives me a discreet vantage point to watch the students.

Monique dryly explains a point of grammar which the students dutifully copy into their notebooks. It all seems so civilized to me, but definitely more staid and formal than my teaching methods.

I look around the classroom. Behind Monique, there is an American flag, a bulletin board, and a 1960's green chalkboard. A filing cabinet near the bank of windows is the only storage in the room. The classroom is stark but functional.

Taking an opportunity to chat with one student at the end of the hour, she shares that the administration is going to "break up the classes," so these students might not have me as a teacher. The student seems very disappointed as I am billed as an exotic teacher: *l'Américaine.*

In the French system, the students travel from class to class in fixed groups, depending on their electives. The students who take challenging courses like science, advanced math, and Spanish or German are in class together; the students who take a standard, less challenging program of study are in a separate grouping. This will have serious repercussions for me, as I will be assigned the latter group.

Once the students are placed in their groups, called "classes", there often is little cross-pollination. Breaking up the classes is significant because the students will find themselves placed in new learning groups.

After class, Monique takes me to the administration building to meet the principal, Madame Laubert.

It is noon.

The reception area is composed of three desks placed in various corners of the room, each one the domain of a secretary. The secretaries are older women, smartly dressed, who greet me with warm, almost motherly, smiles. I will return often to see them during the year, as they are very soothing and kind.

Madame Laubert is a personal friend, if not an accomplice, of Monique. She is in her late fifties approaching retirement.

She has a well-worn tired look on her face. The exaggerated curve of her spine makes her seem old and fragile. There is no wedding ring.

Madame Laubert welcomes me warmly.

"*Bonjour, Madame,*" she begins, continuing in French since she speaks no English. "It is a pleasure to have you with us; you will certainly add a new dimension to our faculty with the new ideas and teaching techniques Monique assures me you have; our teachers will have a lot to learn from you."

I fumble something out of my mouth since I am taken aback at her expectations of me.

"I am sure I will learn a lot this year from my colleagues."

The three of us chat about Bordeaux and the school. Madame Laubert asks me about my family and shows interest in me not only as staff but as a person worth knowing.

In the back of my mind, I wonder why Monique is dawdling as I am looking forward to meeting her colleagues at lunch.

After our chat, we head to the cafeteria and lunchrooms which are across the courtyard from the main classroom building.

We select our meal from the buffet in the cafeteria and proceed to the teachers' dining area. Monique walks briskly past two tables where the majority of teachers are dining. We sit at our own table with two of her friends.

The faculty members at other tables cast glances toward us, but Monique makes no effort to introduce me.

Finally, Monique opens the bottle of wine and offers a glass to the other teachers. At this point, she introduces me to them perfunctorily, then returns to our table.

It is an awkward moment for everyone, and I am disappointed not to have the opportunity to chat with a larger group of teachers.

The meal for students and faculty is the same. It consists of a cold *hors d'oeuvre*, a main course of meat or fish garnished with potato and vegetable, bread, and the option of a sweet dessert or fruit.

The French teachers eat in sequence, first course, second course, and dessert. I eat the hot course first, for in the States, "Eat before your food gets cold" is a dictum we seem to follow. Most of the teachers will let the entrée get cold as they eat their appetizer first, respecting the fixed order of a meal. This is the first insight I have into their Cartesian minds!

We return to her classroom. Monique gives me copies of the three levels of English books to take back with me, plus tapes and workbooks. They are published in Britain and seem, to my American taste, very stuffy.

The terms are quaint. In one dialogue, the mother is "hoovering" under the bed. The accents of the speakers on the tape are heavily British. "Oh, dear me, I cawn't find my glawsses."

In one chapter, an American woman is shopping in the grocery store wearing curlers in her hair: clearly, this British series does not care to show Americans in a favorable light.

The French teachers who teach English speak with a decidedly British accent, as does Monique.

"Really, Jackie, I am delighted your American accent really isn't that bad." I bristle inwardly at the faint praise and think she has seen too many Rocky Balboa movies.

We leave school to return back to Monique's home. I feel reassured now that I have seen my new work world: I will survive.

CHAPTER 8

Getting the Lay of the Land

AFTER THE SCHOOL VISIT, Monique and Jean drive me around the area to give me a feel for the region where I will be living. They drive through a toney community called *la Résidence de St. Pierre* about a mile from the house. The roads, which have romantic names of trees and birds, curve gracefully in arcs and circles around the holes of the golf course. Were it not for the carved wooden street signs, one could get lost, as the streets all look alike.

Jean stops the car in front of a fenced-in property. This house, like its neighbors, is made of stucco and set back on the land, protected by an imposing double gate. Monique pops out of the car and rings the doorbell.

We get out of the car and wait. Eventually, a small, middle-aged woman in white slacks, a khaki blouse and suede house slippers slowly walks down the path from the house to meet us. She looks at me, then my French guides, lifts her hand out of her pocket where she keeps the gate key and lets us in.

"*Bonjour*, Louise. We are just driving around our American, who is going to exchange jobs with me…perhaps I told you? Oh, well, no matter, here she is."

Louise looks at me.

"*Bonjour*," I offer.

She hesitates before trying to piece together some light conversation in this awkward moment.

'Welcome to France," she stammers.

"Thank you. I am happy to be here," I respond with equal awkwardness.

Silence.

She realizes Monique and Jean do not intend to leave.

"Won't you come in? I am just rearranging the kitchen, so things are not as they should be." Her husband, Paul, taller than his wife, is on a ladder replacing a lightbulb in the track lighting. He peers down at us and continues to work.

I am surprised to see the house is contemporary. My first impression from the travertine floors and expanses of floor-to-ceiling windows is the house should be in a modern architecture magazine rather than in this community of traditional stucco houses.

Monique, after a bit of small talk, goes for the attack.

"I'm hoping that while Jackie and Patrick are here, you can have them over, get to know them, you know, that sort of thing."

I counter, to let Louise off the hook, that I suppose she and her husband Paul might be too busy, but perhaps we could meet sometime.

"That would be nice," Louise politely responds.

"We've been to the States a few times, mostly New York and Los Angeles. Loved it," Louise mentions, warming to our presence.

Paul climbs down the ladder, puts the old bulb on the table. He shakes my hand.

"Welcome." He leans against the wall and listens to our small talk.

"Best be getting along, we still have to show Jackie the golf club before dark," Monique announces abruptly.

She marshals us toward the door.

We take our leave. Louise walks us down the long walk to the gate.

40

"Thank you for stopping by," she says politely as she locks the gate.

In the car, Monique implies she just did me a favor, since Louise and Paul are quite the couple to know. Louise and her husband Paul are air traffic controllers at the Bordeaux airport.

I sense Monique is not on social terms with them. It seems to me like a forced entry.

A bit farther down the asphalt road, at the corner, is the entrance to the golf club.

A rustic five-slat wooden sign announces it is the *Golf de St. Pierre.*

We park in the small parking area at the base of a hill and climb the irregular flagstone steps to the clubhouse. It is a two-story, rough-sawn cedar building with a terrace overlooking the putting green and the expanse of fairway leading to the first hole. There is a forest of large trees in the distance. It is definitely a rural club with none of the amenities like reception rooms, formal entry, and well-appointed dining areas one would find in a more elegant club.

The building, with its rustic décor, has the charm of an army barracks.

We read the *carte du jour*, which is posted on a large slate tablet: *omelette aux cèpes et fines herbes, steak frites, poulet garni, vins de Bordeaux en carafe.*

It is classic, simple fare.

Mme Saule, the restaurant manager, is behind the bar. She eyes us carefully as we are not regulars.

Monique addresses her, "We are here with the American who is going to be living in the area and who loves golf."

The promise of a new diner quickens her interest.

"Ah, then we will see a lot of you. Welcome. I can give you the name of the membership chairman. It will be easy to join, and I think you will like it.

We have a ladies' golf group; you will get to know people quite quickly."

I invite Jean and Monique to sit and have a glass of wine on the terrace, but Monique turns down the offer.

"Come now. Let's get back. I have to prepare dinner."

I leave reluctantly since, despite the simple décor, I feel like this is going to be a safe, go-to spot when Patrick and I need to get out.

August

CHAPTER 9

Training for the Job

THE INTERNATIONAL TEACHER EXCHANGE Program holds orientation meetings at the American University, in Washington D.C., in mid-August.

During the orientation, American exchange teachers and their foreign partners attend training sessions together to learn the ins and outs of the program and what their legal and professional responsibilities are while teaching abroad in their new work environment. Also, time is allotted for partners to dialogue about their respective schools.

The accompanying spouses, partners, and children also have a few programs for their orientation, but mostly, they tour the Washington area together while the exchange teachers are in meetings.

Monique and Jean and the children fly in the night before from France to attend the first scheduled meetings. They meet us at breakfast.

"So good to see you. How was your flight? Any problems? Are you tired?" I ask.

"No, of course not," Monique bristles.

I look around the cafeteria at the other American teachers with their counterparts.

It is interesting to see the dynamics of these newly formed

teams. Some look like they have known each other forever, chatting easily, and others are awkward, like on a first date.

Monique is tense and critical of the schedule of meetings.

"I really don't think we need all of this. It would be nice to visit the city as well."

We have a menu of meetings to select from which we decide to attend together:

What Every Exchange Teacher Needs to Know

Getting your Resident Visa

Dealing with Medical Emergencies

To Exchange Cars: Pros and Cons

How to Handle Discipline Problems

Monique and I have time to talk about lesson planning and the rules and culture of our respective schools.

But it is as if we are talking right past each other. It is easy to talk about the respective school schedules, vacations, and parent conference meetings; however, it seems impossible for each of us to communicate to each other the true essence of our teaching jobs.

I struggle to convey what my relationship is like with my students, that my students need to be challenged, yet gently nurtured.

"The students are accustomed to a setting where the teacher is not the master, but a coach who encourages their progress through kindness and by demonstrating warm concern. You also have to make them laugh. They love that."

I go on to say that in my classes, there is not an "I-Thou" relationship of a teacher pronouncing from on high. An authoritative attitude does not work with my American students.

To get the students to take risks speaking French, the ambiance in the classroom has to be relaxed, or they will not feel comfortable making mistakes, which is a necessary part of their learning.

Monique's eyes glaze over. She has no notion of what I am saying.

From what I have observed, there is an invisible glass wall between her and her students. At best, a few sarcastic, quippy remarks is the only humor I detect when I watch her teach. Maybe this is the French way.

I have hope that somehow, once in my school, she is going to miraculously loosen up, by becoming a quick study and talking to my colleagues.

But how would she treat my tender Ana?

Basically, I am praying for a personality transplant.

Monique, for her part, emphasizes her students need to be kept orderly and obedient. That the discipline system at the school is poorly defined because Madame Tabata, a fiery, volatile woman, is inconsistent in her policies, so I will be on my own.

Monique goes through the litany of colleagues I will meet, outlining their weaknesses and quirks. One is a depressive, another is seemingly nice but can criticize you behind your back, another thinks he is a great teacher but is not. It seems, apart from one or two, she is suspicious of them all.

I take notes, so I will know who the cast of characters are when I meet them, but I doubt they can all be that bad.

Monique speaks of the principal, Madame Laubert, whom I met in June as someone she likes very much. Monique tells me I can depend on her to be a good listener, but Monsieur Girard, the vice-principal, really runs the show. Monique then adds the faculty do not like or trust either of them.

Almost too much information!

How am I going to interact with these obviously flawed people? The positive impression I had of the school after my visit in June is radically changed. After Monique's description, I fear that what had seemed like a well-run, tidy little school is, in reality, very disorganized.

During the training in Washington, I am still dazzled by the dream of going to France and submerge my misgivings beneath the excitement of this new French life.

It is summed up by the name tag I proudly wear:

Jacqueline Donnelly – France

CHAPTER 10

Interlude

AT THE END OF the meetings, the International Exchange team sends us off to all parts of the world, wishing us all a wonderful adventure in our new schools.

Patrick and I suggest to Monique and Jean they might enjoy taking a week to sightsee, since they plan to drive to Michigan from Washington.

This interlude before their arrival allows Patrick and me to savor our last days at home and gives us time to pack and organize the house for our departure. We also want to plan a welcome party for Monique and Jean and the kids so they will know neighbors and friends and not feel alone.

Monique is annoyed I am not leaving for France from Washington but choose to return home for a week or so before departure. She wants the house immediately to themselves.

I do not want to leave right away.

If I go to France immediately after the meeting, I will have to spend three weeks before school without my husband as he cannot join me until later. This idea does not appeal to me as I am not in a hurry to leave my home and friends any sooner than I have to since it will be nine months before I am allowed to return the United States according to my teacher contract.

Perhaps the program is afraid if I return, I will not want to go back again.

Summer also is the best time in our beautiful town, which abuts the sandy beaches of Lake Michigan. A channel connects the large lake to a small inland lake, affording opportunities for boating, swimming, and waterskiing. Magnificent houses line the shores of both lakes. I love it and want to linger a bit.

And to say Monique's house is in a rural setting is accurate. I am used to living in a city or a suburb. Their home is located in a small cluster of houses located on one side of a tar road.

Across the street from Monique's house, a barbed wire fence protects a field where, at dusk, the cows in an adjoining pasture come to the edge to socialize. This is the area's nightlife.

When Patrick joins me, I am sure we will enjoy it, but for now, there would not be much to do for a woman alone.

While Monique and her family are driving through upper New York and Canada, Patrick and I busy ourselves phoning banks, changing addresses, setting aside documents we might need in France, and making the last reluctant preparations for departure. As motivated as we are to start this adventure, there is a sentimental tug in our hearts about leaving.

After only a few days of travel, the French family arrives...home.

Monique and Jean and the kids settle into our lower level, which overlooks the lake, for our last few days together.

To celebrate their new American way of life, we organize a picnic with our neighbors and some of Monique's future colleagues.

We order a three-foot-long Subway sandwich, garnished with coleslaw and potato salads, chips, pickles, and condiments laid out on a red and white checkered tablecloth.

As Monique and Jean meet their new friends, Jennifer and Roger bond with kids their own age, soon disappearing for walks in the woods.

The atmosphere on that sunny summer day is festive and classic picnic-Americana.

The laughter and happy talk assure us the French family is going to feel a part of the neighborhood.

Gathering in the dining room, we present Monique and Roger with a two-tier chocolate sheet cake.

The decoration is perfect for the occasion: Mickey Mouse, in a little yellow plastic airplane, flying the span of the cake from "France" to the "U.S.A."

The plastic Mickey will travel with us to France and be set on our mantel. I will look at it throughout the year - sometimes affectionately - and sometimes suspecting it is more symbolic than I originally thought.

Monique and Jean see our friends to the door.

They hear encouraging words:

"Just call us if you need anything. We are so excited you are here. You are going to love the town."

Patrick and I are pleased the picnic is a success.

This party makes us confident Monique will know people who can support her, and with whom she can have some fun, and the family will not feel like strangers in a strange land.

CHAPTER 11

And They're Off!

FINALLY, THE BIG DAY arrives. It is time to leave.

Beth, who is 21, and about to return to college as a senior in mid-September, suggested to me weeks before that she accompany me to Bordeaux to help me get settled.

"I really think you need me, Mom. We can open up the house, get settled, and enjoy Bordeaux for a while."

While Beth knows she will be a help, she also sees this as a great mini-French vacation.

I relish her company and look forward to time alone with my daughter. Soon she will be off starting her life, and these opportunities may no longer be available.

We have breakfast with Monique and Jean for the last time, gingerly stepping over our suitcases lined up like building blocks in the hall.

We wedge four suitcases, and two carry-on bags, into the trunk of the car. I linger to look at our home, the plantings we saved to landscape the exterior, the dent in the garage where Beth tried to park the car years ago, the lake peeking out in the distance, and think how lucky Monique and her family are to stay in my home.

The lake glistens in the sun, flashing streaks of light through the windows; the boughs of the trees nod up and down as the breeze swirls through their branches.

Why are we leaving? It is so safe here. The walls of the house seem to encircle us like the arms of our mother, nestling us in soft familiarity, reluctant to let us go.

We sense Monique is mentally toe-tapping an impatient rhythm in her mind, "When will they leave, when will they go?"

The family walks Beth and me to the car.

A few mechanical hugs and *bon voyages*.

"Don't forget to look up our friends. And keep the shutters closed!" Monique insists.

Patrick backs out of the driveway. I look back at our home for the last time.

We wave to Jean, Roger, and Jennifer.

Monique has already turned her back and walked into the house.

We are off. I have gone to France many times, on vacation with Patrick, or leading students on two-week tours of the Loire Valley, Normandy, and Brittany, but I always returned after a brief sojourn.

This time I am going to live and work there. It is difficult to wrap my mind around the finality of it all. No regrets – rather, great excitement - but respectful of the enormous decision I have made.

On the Air France flight from Chicago to Paris, we befriend the flight attendants in our section, explaining I am going to France to teach for a year and am looking forward to this new adventure. I tell them I dearly love France and treasure the opportunity to live there like a French person, not a tourist. This touches their hearts. Word spreads among the crew. Each attendant approaches us to furtively slip us splits of wine and champagne. What we don't drink we stuff in our travel bag.

We disembark to hugs and well wishes from the flight crew, the bottles of wine clinking as they jostle one another in our carry-on bags.

After a short layover in Paris, we board the plane for Bordeaux. A bit jet-lagged, Beth naps on the plane. Her long brown hair drapes her neck, her brown eyes hidden by heavy eyelids; her clear, fresh complexion gives her an angelic look.

I look at her, my beloved daughter, sleeping peacefully, as she did as a child.

It is a momentary reprieve from the passing of time: a glimpse back to the child who is no longer. She is now my adult daughter and a dear friend, a travel companion, sharing these moments with me.

CHAPTER 12

The Arrival

MONIQUE ARRANGES FOR HER friend, Catherine, to meet us at the airport and drive us to the house. Catherine is a good-natured, rotund woman with curly ginger hair carefully cropped to her head, wearing tan slacks, a lavender blouse patterned with tiny purple flowers like those found on wallpaper, sensible shoes, and a beige jacket. She waves to us through the glass partition which separates travelers from the outside world as we retrieve our bags from the carousel.

"*Bonjour*" Her words are muffled as she kisses us on each cheek and takes one of our suitcases.

She breaks into English knowing we are weary; Catherine teaches English in a neighboring high school and is very proud of her skill. She speaks a lovely but somewhat stiff English.

Exiting the passenger terminal, we pass a fifteen-foot plastic inflated bottle of wine advertising *Cheval Blanc* poised in the center of a causeway. We are indeed in wine country.

Catherine drives us to the rental car area where I present my paperwork for a pre-paid *Mégane*, a green sedan with soft brown leather seats and a new car smell, which we have leased for the year.

"The insurance papers and your car registration are in the glove compartment; you will need to fill up the tank," the agent cautions us.

The arrow on the dashboard is on the far side of empty. As we follow Catherine, my eyes dart down nervously at the gauge as we weave through two lanes of heavy traffic.

"Beth, my lord, what if we run out of gas? This is really stupid. Can't they have left us with more than this?"

"Relax, Mom, we are going to make it."

To our relief, Catherine signals us to exit right to a small service station.

"*Faites le plein,*" I tell the attendant since the tank is beyond empty. As the numbers on the pump speed upward, my stomach releases its grip.

While I follow Catherine across the *Pont Aquitaine,* Beth programs the radio.

We have our heart set on a quick trip, a fast goodbye, and a good nap in our new home.

Being hospitable and very French, Catherine reasons we want nothing more than to enjoy a hearty meal in her home.

Catherine and her family hail from Alsace, the easternmost province bordering the Rhine River. Because of the Germanic influence, the cuisine is rich and heavy.

For starters, we have sausages, pickles, and relishes. A thick, tomato-based beef stew follows, laden with potatoes and carrots. She serves a cheese tray of regional French cheeses before presenting us with a layered cheesecake.

Beth and I, lightly suffering from a copious tasting of wine on the plane, manage to eat the fare so as to not disappoint Catherine, her husband, Thomas, and her two sons, who eye us cautiously.

After the meal, over coffee and chocolates in the living room, we visit a bit more.

With a theatrical yawn, I suggest Beth and I should get some rest. We follow Catherine and her husband through country roads flanked by vineyards to the roundabout which will take us through the commercial area of Saint Pierre.

We pass a shopping center, which is closed, being Sunday. The road narrows, passing village houses. On the right, we can see a large stone château defined by two conical towers on either side of the three-story fortress. As we drive, our eye catches the *TGV*, the rapid train, speeding to Paris like a zephyr. The contrast of medieval and modern seems to be symbolic of France today.

The road winds past a dilapidated barn with one side of the roof collapsed, guarded by an old man perched on a bale of hay watching us pass, his head turning in an arc from left to right, monitoring our progress until we fade out of view.

Finally, at the white-washed stone fence, Catherine and Thomas turn left onto a single paved road. I recognize Monique's house by the gate.

Monique has given Catherine the keys to the house.

We disembark from our car, extract the suitcases from the trunk, and follow our guides into the house.

We find a service light in the entry, which is enough to illuminate our passage into the cavern-like house. Having been closed up for weeks, the house has a faint aroma of meals past.

Thomas opens the shutters one by one. The late golden afternoon sun filters in with each window liberated from the darkness, revealing piecemeal the tidy home Monique and Jean have left for us.

Monique has left me a note of welcome, a spare set of keys to the house, and the keys to my classroom.

We walk Catherine and Thomas to the car.

"Thank you, Catherine. So sweet of you to take care of us. We will call when we get settled and have you all over. *Au revoir!*"

We watch as the sedan pulls out of the driveway. We close the door. We are finally alone.

We did it!

Journey's end.

CHAPTER 13

Home at Last

BETH AND I ABANDON the suitcases in the living room and flee to our bedrooms where we nestle under the duvets for a restorative nap.

The departure from home, the flight to Paris, the connection to Bordeaux, our arrival, Catherine's welcome, followed by the heavy family meal are a jumble in our minds. How could all of this have happened in one single day?

It is dark when I awake from the nap. Where am I? I feel like a disoriented traveler in a strange hotel room.

Fumbling for a light, I get my bearings, and then go gently wake my daughter.

Beth and I are hungry. Naturally, there are no provisions in the house so we leave, locking and checking the doors several times to make sure all will be safe upon our return.

We turn onto the road following the route we took a few hours back. In the black velvet darkness, our headlights guide us on unfamiliar narrow roads.

We drive past the commercial center, through the next town; nothing is open.

Continuing on for 20 minutes, we see an illuminated billboard advertising the Carrefour hypermarket, one of the larger food chains in France. Below the signage is an arrow pointing us to the highway.

Driving on, trusting the arrow, which is our North Star, we find the welcoming lights of the large market. Ten minutes until closing! Beth and I run into the store like contestants on a grab-all shopping spree and fill our baskets with anything we can reach before the witching hour and we are chased out.

Miraculously we find our way home again.

We populate the cabinets with pasta, sauces, chips, the refrigerator with cheeses, fruit, salads, and meat.

Sinking into the leather sofa in the living room, we open two splits of Bordeaux wine.

"Here's to you, Beth. Cheers!"

"Cheers, Mom. We did it!"

We clink our glasses, jubilant to have survived Day One.

We sleep deliciously in the darkness provided by the re-fastened shutters until Catherine calls at 9:00 a.m. to see if all is well.

CHAPTER 14

Getting Settled

"Yes, we are fine, thank you, Catherine. How sweet of you to call. Of course, we will let you know if we need anything. Thanks again, bye now."

I am so annoyed. I was in the deepest sleep I had in days when the phone rang.

Getting up quietly so as not to disturb Beth in the other room, I go to the kitchen to make coffee.

Coffee. Where the hell is the coffee pot? There is no coffee pot. O.K., we bought instant coffee. I will just boil some water in a saucepan and be done with it.

Saucepan. Where is it?

I see it in the back of the cabinet. To reach it, I remove a large cauldron and lid, which I put on the counter. It seems heavy. I discover it is filled with rancid cooking oil Monique has preserved for future use. Disgusting. I put the lid back on the pot to prevent the stench from filling the kitchen.

I will deal with this later. I need coffee.

I fill the small saucepan with water and place it on the burner. Turning the dial on the stove, nothing happens. Nothing. Now this is getting really annoying.

No coffee maker, no gas, please, someone, help me.

I notice a little valve above the cooktop, which I remember in a memory-flash is the spigot to turn on the gas.

Turning the dial again, the electric starter ignites the gas. I boil the water impatiently hovering over the pan, anticipating the welcome jolt of caffeine to get me started.

Carrying my cup to the garden, I take in the view. In the soft, mid-August morning, the warm breeze jostles the trees that line the garden, the leaves sway in unison like a *corps de ballet,* creating a backdrop for the jet blue sky above.

I walk the pebble path around the planting area, admiring the golden strawflowers peeking out below the circle of verdant shrubbery.

My feet crackle on the little stones as I walk to the low wall that delineates the property from the road.

Efficient little cars speed by en route to seemingly important destinations, nonplussed by the woman in her long silk robe leisurely sipping her coffee as she strolls.

Turning back toward the patio, I spy our neighbors across the fence. I certainly do not want to meet them this way, so I duck into the kitchen for shelter.

Beth joins me in the kitchen to receive a tutorial on how to make coffee.

"So where should we go this morning?" she asks.

"Let's check out the shopping center to see what's what."

After another cup of coffee, dressed for the day, I gingerly back the car out of the garage. Beth and I can see the neighbors have two small boys in tow and are about to pile into the car. I lower the window.

"*Bonjour,*" I proffer timidly. My greeting is met warmly by the mother, Diane, who strides over to the fence separating our properties and extends her hand.

"Welcome! Monique told us you would be here for the year. Alex, come here." Summoned, her husband leaves the children in the car and joins Diane to greet us.

Diane, who is in her late thirties, has a rapid rhythm to her mirthful speech. She is stocky without being heavy, sharp green eyes complementing her auburn hair.

She has a slight gap between her first two teeth that makes her smile disarming.

Alex, a bit taller than his wife, pushes his coal-black hair peppered with strands of grey back from his face with his hand.

Alex drives a bus part-time in the city of Bordeaux, allowing him to watch the children while Diane works three days a week as a nurse's aide.

"Why not come over for a drink tonight, say at 5? We would like to welcome you to the neighborhood," Diane says.

Beth and I accept our first invitation in our new home. This is the first crack in the ice. Now we will know someone in Bordeaux!

CHAPTER 15

Girls Get Hungry Too,
You Know

OFF WE GO TO the Super U grocery store, the small hypermarket, which anchors the nearby shopping center. An enormous white sign with the words SUPER U in blue and red is perched on the roof. It is lit day and night like a beacon.

We park the car in the angled parking area, walk to the grocery cart area, and try to extract a cart. Pulling hard, we drag ten, which are tethered together, toward us. A few people glance our way.

"What's the deal?" Beth asks.

Dropping back, we watch a seasoned shopper put a coin in the slot, releasing the chain connecting one cart to another.

"Oh, I get it," I say. Both of us feel like aliens on our first day on earth. *Can't we even get a grocery cart out successfully?*

We slowly peruse each aisle, examining cans, boxes, bottles, sometimes familiar, often exotic, wondering at times what the contents are since our food-French is lacking. Were it not for the pictures on some items, we would have no clue.

We lose ourselves in the cheese section. Posters of happy-faced cows indicate which region the cheese comes from. I remember the quote of De Gaulle: "How can anyone govern a nation that has two hundred and forty-six different kinds of cheese?" Many French people can identify at a glance many varieties, where they come from, and they know how to pair them with wine.

The wine department has a particular appeal. We walk down three aisles displaying bottles of red, white, rosé, and Sauternes, some with plain labels, others touting logos of fine wineries in Bordeaux and beyond. It seems weird to be drinking Bordeaux as a domestic wine when it is so exotic in the States.

The glassy-eyed cashier, seated at a swivel stool, passes our selections under a scanner. The groceries are piling up at the end of the conveyor belt. I forget we are supposed to bag our own groceries. The cashier slides down plastic bags for us to use when she realizes we have not brought our own.

We are happy to see a screen which indicates what we have to pay; I count out the francs carefully, avoiding the coins, as I have not used them for a while and can't remember their value.

Exiting the market, we spot the *boulangerie* on the right. We are enticed by the aroma of the freshly baked bread. Waiting our turn, we observe from the shelves behind the vendor that among our choices are a baguette, *demi-baguette, pain de campagne, pain de mie*, or if we want something sweeter, a brioche bread. We point to a baguette and two croissants. The white-aproned lady puts the croissants into a toffee-colored square of paper and spins both ends three times to close it.

She slides the baguette into a cylindrical paper bag; the temptation to eat the pointed end is too much for us. As we exit the store, we slide the bread out of the bag. Beth and I each eat an end. The crust crackles, the crumbs fall onto our clothing. We savor the white, porous, baked dough, hungry for the next bite. We take the maimed bread with our other groceries and put them in the car.

Next to the supermarket is a small brasserie, consisting of seven tables. The wall is covered with photos of soccer stars from the Bordeaux team *Les Girondins,* named after the estuary separating the city port from the Atlantic. The plastic ashtrays bear the names of liqueurs. In the center of each table is a cruet of oil and vinegar and a little pot of Dijon mustard.

The menu is classic: baked chicken and fries, steak and fries, fish and fries, sausage and fries, each accompanied by a green salad in a vinaigrette sauce. How can we lose?

The raspy-voiced woman, well into her sixties, who takes our order, disappears into the kitchen. She returns to flirt with the regulars.

'Hey, Jean, what is going on?" "Pierre, the same as always?" In the other room, in an alcove, men in blue overalls hover over small glasses of whiskey. The smoke from the room and the odor of stale beer waft into the restaurant, but we pay it no mind, as we are nestled in a booth.

We order lunch, sharing a *pichet* of red wine with an apple tarte chaser.

Victoire!

CHAPTER 16

As We Go A' Wandering

AFTER LUNCH, WE TAKE off to wander about. Like Hansel and
Gretel leaving breadcrumbs, we memorize the features of land-
marks, the grey stone house, the weathered barn, and the fountain
at the roundabout which should help us find our way home

We set out on a double lane highway toward the next town of
Saint-Vincent. On each side of the road are random storefronts: a
beauty salon, travel agency, and hardware shop placed in between
modest houses. The focal point of the town, dominating the main
square, is the grey stone church with a single spire.

We park the car and take the stone path on the far side of the
church to the parish cemetery. Sepulchers line each path, the
engraving on many eroded by the elements. On the vertical grave-
stones, oval photos of the departed beneath carved inscriptions give
us insights into the people who walked our paths long ago. Men
with stiff white-collared shirts, round glasses, and stern looks beneath the words, "Dearest Father." Women whose hair is piled high
in a washerwoman style, lace-ruffled collars centered with a broach
or cameo: "Our beautiful Mother" or a child in a gossamer shirt
with unkempt curly hair: "Taken from us too soon."

Dried, neglected chrysanthemums, faded plastic flowers in
green pots, remnants of family visits in times past, litter some of the

gravesites.

The French decidedly do not make verdant parks out of their cemeteries as we do.

Across the street is a U-shaped strip mall. Spindly metal frames placed in the open area await market day when the merchants will drape the supports with canvas and install tables for their wares of fruits, vegetables, fish, and flowers.

Brocanteurs are the people who will unpack, try to sell, and repack assorted family possessions, old records, postcards, random forks, knives and spoons, and photos of people in tarnished frames on market day. And the *chineurs,* the people who love these market-type garage sales, know the vendors and barter playfully for their wares.

Aside from the bank, the pharmacy, and the cleaners, the star of the commercial center is one of the rare restaurants in the area, Pizza Napoli.

Diners have the option of taking their meal inside the restaurant or outside on a small terrace at round café tables draped with faded red-checked cloths. The white paper napkins are tethered by ashtrays. Round bottomed wine glasses are inverted over red ruffled-edged placemats, which sport advertising for local businesses.

Convinced we have scoped out the area, we reverse our route, driving in the opposite direction to vineyards.

We have never been close to vines before, so we turn onto a one-lane road, passing from one vineyard to the next.

We park along the side of a road, walk down a gulley, and up again to inspect close hand the maple tree-like leaves and the plump, dusty-purple grapes which are draped on parallel wires supported by posts.

Bees dart between the leaves on their appointed daily rounds; the birds sing in competition with the soft, irregular buzz of the highway, which is faint in the distance.

The sun's warmth on our backs, the sticky residue on our fingers, the dust on our shoes, are tender initiations into our new rural life.

This is *le Bordelais,* the lush, fertile region outside the city of Bordeaux.

Picking a handful of grapes, we pop them in our mouths, savoring the sweet-tart flavor.

We decide it is time to go back and settle in, unpack our clothing, and make this house our home.

"No, I think you made a right at the corner here," Beth says.

"Are you sure we didn't drive past this farmhouse?"

"Nope, I would have remembered it," she responds.

Ceding to Beth, who is younger and often more alert, I follow her directions.

Finding the highway again, we pass a young woman carrying a shopping bag. She is walking with the brisk, assured step of someone who is on a mission.

"No, this isn't right, let's turn back," I suggest. We turn around and drive back.

We pass the woman again as she walks resolutely.

"Are you sure you know where we are going? Let's go back to the city hall and start over again."

We pass the woman again.

"How are we going to get back? I am out of ideas."

Beth guesses we did not make the turn a quarter mile ahead and that was our error.

As we pass the woman again, she stares at us in wonder as to what we are up to.

"You're right. Here is the service road we missed."

Enfin! At last, we are home!

We arrive a bit after 5:00 p.m. at our neighbors' house for cocktails. We do not want to appear too anxious, although it is the highlight of the day for us.

Diane greets us warmly as if we have been friends for years. Entering the small vestibule, we follow her into the living-dining area. The look is quite contemporary contrasted to Monique's traditional house: green leather couches, a glass coffee table with shiny aluminum legs, a variegated ivy plant cascading down a wooden étagère. There are two picture windows. One window looks out onto a view of the pasture and the other to the vineyards.

Alex has arranged a display of liqueurs and wines on the coffee table from which to choose. Ricard, the anise-flavored syrup, a favorite to be mercifully diluted with soda water or plain water; bitter Martini and Rossi, deceptively sounding like the martini cocktail; and a bottle of red, and one of white, wine.

Beth and I opt for the safe road and sip a white Bordeaux, as does Diane. Alex pours himself a generous glass of Ricard.

"So, where in the States are you from, exactly? When is your husband coming? Have you been to France before?" These questions prime the evening's conversation.

The boys, Stephane and Pierre, dart in to give us a brief *Bonsoir* before resuming their soccer game in the grassy area beyond the kitchen.

We nibble on mixed nuts, radishes, and olives as we drink our second glass of wine.

Diane is a font of practical information and advice, counseling us where to buy the best meat and produce. She cautions that very few bakeries have bread up to her expectations.

We leave an hour or so later, walking around the decorative fence which informally delineates our properties, to our dark house.

Diane and Alex stay at their door to make sure we have no problems re-entering, wave, and yell, "À *bientôt.*"

We are thrilled to know they are nearby and will see them soon.

CHAPTER 17

Laying Down Roots

IN LATE AUGUST, AS many French are still on holiday, the atmosphere in the village is relaxed. The cafés are filled with people basking in the late summer sun. Friends are leisurely sipping their wine, nibbling on Kalamata olives and nuts, and many, smoking their cigarettes under Cinzano umbrellas. Single diners read books or newspapers, while others idly watch the traffic pass by.

Beth and I are in the same mood. I still have time before school officially starts, and although teacher orientation days are approaching, I still feel as if I am on vacation. How lucky I am to be living in France!

"Beth, let's not cook tonight. I think I can find the golf club."

La Résidence de St. Pierre is mercifully well-marked. Streets serpentine around the fairways, but at every intersection a signpost with an arrow points to our destination.

It is Friday night, and the club parking lot is full. We find a spot on the street.

The terrace and restaurant are buzzing with people drinking after their round of golf.

Madame Saule recognizes me when I enter. "*Ah, la petite Américaine!*" I am very tall, but the word *petite* is a term of endearment the French use to convey familiarity.

"Madame, this is my daughter Beth. We would like a table for dinner."

"Ah, you do not want to eat alone!"

Taking me by the hand, she leads me to the side dining room where the regulars are assembled.

"Everyone, welcome (turning to me, she asks our names) Jackie and her daughter, Beth. She is from America and will be with us for the school year."

A couple still wearing their golf hats motion to two empty seats, "Please join us!"

We sit down. We are integrated immediately into the conversation.

"Do you play golf. Are you going to join the club?" Answering affirmatively to both, our dining partners seem pleased.

Beth, who speaks a correct but slightly hesitant French, understands enough to respond politely to their questions.

The thread of the conversation returns to the missed putt or the birdie on hole *Trois*.

It is a *prix fixe* meal. For the first course, we are served individual plates of a speckled *pâté* of onion, capers, herbs, and ground beef. A brimming basket of French bread is placed at every third person's place.

A ruddy-faced man, who sits at the head of the table, rises to address the gathering, tapping a glass to get our attention.

"*Mes amis*, we have a large turnout tonight for our end-of-summer meal.

We will meet again in a few weeks to celebrate the start of the grape harvest.

Pierre, fill us in. When do you think it will be?"

Pierre, who owns a vineyard near St Émilion, rises to answer the question.

"As you know the exact moment of the grape harvest is like the

Second Coming. We will not know the time! The master vintners are, as always, seriously studying the weather. The grapes look good this year, close to their peak, yet a hailstorm could do us in."

The diners mumble "*Certainement*" as they remember past years when sudden storms destroyed acres of vines.

"So, I cannot say for certain but let's make a toast to Les *Vendanges* 1999."

The clinking of glasses left and right unites the diners.

Continuing with the feast, waiters arrive bearing large white ceramic platters of *confit de canard,* duck thighs arranged symmetrically around the perimeter of the dishes, garnished with field greens in the center.

Waiters skillfully serve the meat with two large forks.

Deep round bowls of scalloped potatoes and green beans are to be passed family-style. The plates and bowls circulate more than once.

The empty bottles of wine are quickly replaced.

It feels like a medieval Robin Hood banquet.

For dessert, we indulge in a golden flan with a dollop of snow-white cream.

We linger with the group, trying to memorize faces if not names for the next visit.

This evening means so much to me. It is good to be reminded that when Beth leaves, Patrick and I will have a gathering place where we will be welcome.

It would be lovely to think this hiatus before school begins could last forever, that I could live in France savoring an endless summer, but it is not to be.

CHAPTER 18

It Doesn't Get Better Than This

PATRICK FINALLY ARRIVES IN Bordeaux. Our new life officially starts when we are together again.

Driving back from the Merignac airport, Beth and I regale him
with stories of how we have been spending our days, the gaffes
we have made, and, above all, how proud we are to now feel like
natives.

Since Patrick has never seen the house, we give him the grand
tour. We have removed the vases of artificial flowers and the endless
knickknacks we found on tables and shelves, packing them carefully away in a storage area. The house is filled with fresh flowers.

Patrick tours the house and remarks it was clearly built for shorter people, as he cannot fully stand under the staircase nor in Jean and Monique's loft bedroom, too low for his 6'2" frame. For this reason, we sleep in the first-floor guest bedroom.

After spending a day getting settled, Patrick is ready for the trip Beth and I have planned to the city of St Émilion, known for its world-class wine.

We take the rural route from the house to the highway Beth and I now know very well, en route to Libourne, the capital of the wine trade from ages past, where ships from England and beyond would dock to fill their holds with the best the region had to offer.

From Libourne, we take the N-89 to St Émilion. The two-way highway is dotted by billboards touting the sale of local wines. Small storefronts with limited parking offer free tastings. On both sides of the highway are rolling hills and vineyards, protected by curved stonewalls delineating the property.

Approaching St Émilion, we can see the imposing bell tower of the monolithic church from a distance. We turn off the highway, following a road; the same road, we suppose, that could have been used by the Romans in the fourth century, who, according to tradition, planted the first grapes. Or, this route might have been taken by Émilian, an eighth-century Benedictine monk who directed the carving out of caves and caverns, which were ideal for the fermenting and aging of wine.

But today it is our turn to discover St Émilion, and we are very excited to visit the city.

Parking in a lower level lot, we walk up a cobblestone path to the city center. We wander the small streets, which all seem uphill no matter what the direction. Tempting us at every turn are modern, high-end wine stores, offering private tastings of St Émilion, Pomerol, Moules, and Pauillac wines; delicatessens selling *foie gras*, *pâté* and regional conserves; and of course, the tourist shops filled with trinkets, postcards, wine openers, and aprons.

The weather on this early September day is delicious. It is summer-warm, bright, with a light wind nudging the clouds by.

We choose an outdoor café close to the city center in the shadow of the massive grey stone church. We are lured in by the rectangular chalkboard announcing the entrées, *plats du jour*, and desserts.

We sit under a canvas canopy at a large wooden slat table, with crimson placemats and sparkling wine glasses.

To start, we decide on succulent melons ripened to summer sweetness, wrapped in a luscious slice of Parma ham; we add warm goat cheese toasts to share.

For his *plat principal*, Patrick chooses duck à *l'orange*, accompanied by herb rice, and the early, slender string beans called *primeurs*. Beth and I succumb to the grilled beef in a bordelaise sauce, fries, and a green salad. The crispy crust, soft-centered, French bread is, as ever, perfect for soaking up every drop of the remaining sauce.

We order a bottle of *Château Figeac* to complement the meal. Reasoning we will eat light that night, we enjoy a thin apple tart for dessert.

I look at Patrick and Beth sitting against a backdrop of verdant vineyards and think how fortunate we are to be together in such an idyllic setting and how fortunate I am to live for a year in Bordeaux.

I just have to teach, and it will be, from what I saw on my visit last June, not difficult to do. It is a fair trade for the pleasure of life in France.

September

CHAPTER 19

A Visit to Mom and Dad

MONIQUE HAS ARRANGED FOR us to visit her parents, who live 45 minutes away from our home.

Beth, who has a keen interest in wines, is looking forward to meeting Monique's father who just retired as president of their local wine cooperative.

I am eager to meet Monique's mother; Monique has mentioned she is apprehensive about Monique and her family living so far away. I hope to reassure her during our visit that they will be fine.

We are invited to arrive at 2:00 p.m.

We are greeted by her mother, Elise, and her father, Edouard.

We are escorted into the small living room. Sunlight filters through intricate lace curtains hung on a thick, round brass rod. Two settees face each other with wing chairs on either side. I cast a glance at the bronze-framed family photos arranged on the shelves of the dark mahogany breakfront, placed in between a flowered soup tureen and decorative vases.

The pictures are of Monique, Jean, and the children on vacation; great-grandparents in stiff poses from generations past; and a photo of Edouard, as a slender soldier in his khaki uniform, smiling beside his jeep. And one, that I guess is Elise, on her wedding day, looking down dreamily at her bouquet.

She no longer resembles that young woman. Time has widened her girth, her face is fuller, and the long locks have been cut into a short grey bob.

Elise is dressed conservatively in a powder blue skirt, white silk blouse, and a blue jacket adorned with a pearl pin. She wears shiny hose and squat black heels.

Edouard, still slight, wears double pleated grey slacks, a crisp white shirt, and a burgundy wool tie tucked into his grey, three-button V-neck cardigan.

They have set out a tray of assorted packaged cookies and a sliced fruit cake.

We are offered orange juice or pineapple juice.

Elise elects to sit in the wing chair closest to us.

After some pleasantries, Elise says, "I do miss my daughter, Jean and the children. We so loved seeing them every Sunday for dinner."

She adds, "The last time I saw Monique is when she dropped off her jewelry, china and good silver to us for safekeeping."

I bristle interiorly, as we left all of our fine china and sterling for Monique's use.

She continues, "I worry so much about them. They are so far away. There is so much that could happen."

Edouard interjects, "*Mais non, chérie,* they will be fine."

I sense this is a worry she expresses regularly, and Edouard now, automatically, parries it with reassurances.

As she talks, Elise twists her worn gold wedding band around her finger.

I assure them both we live in a lovely area, that it is safe, and the negative news reported on television about crime in big American cities is not what happens in our little town.

"Oh, but they are so far away. I just worry."

Beth interjects she is interested in wine.

Edouard takes his cue to change the subject, and the conversation wanders to the local wines and wine production.

Elise rises to refill our glasses then retires to the kitchen for a few moments, since she is no longer directing the conversation toward her anxieties.

Returning, Elise waits for a pause in the conversation to grill us on Monique's life in the States.

I imagine she knows all of the details from Monique but wants a second rendition to see if Monique is telling true.

Despite Edouard's cordial bearing, there is a tension in the living room due to Elise's fearful attitude.

From what I observe, Monique is very like Elise, both being rather cautious and suspicious. However, unlike Elise, Monique and Jean are more risk-takers since they have chosen to live in a new environment.

Why did they choose to do this? Was Monique seeking a new adventure or fleeing something that does not work for her in France?

Was something at the school unpleasant, or might she just wish to create a little space between her parents and her family?

I may find clues throughout the year which could answer my questions.

We take our leave and return to St. Pierre, having done our social duty.

I wanted to offer to be family for Elise and Edouard, to fill the void their daughter's leaving created, but it is clear, as the door closes to their home, it is closed to us as well.

CHAPTER 20

There is No Turning Back Now

THE THREE OF US continue to savor our life in the Bordeaux area.

We sip coffee on the terrace in the morning, deliberating how we will spend our last days before I start work.

Mark calls from Japan, where he is working, to see how we are faring. Mark speaks a relaxed, conversational French and has traveled with us to France several times, so he can well imagine how delighted we are to be spending these lazy days before Beth leaves and I begin to work.

"Drink some *rouge* for me, please. Looking forward to seeing you at Christmas!"

In and around Bordeaux, there are so many wonderful temptations, so many inviting places we can go, pretending we are French locals enjoying the richness of the wine region.

There is a *château* near our home surrounded by extensive geometric gardens in the shadow of its ramparts. We wander the grounds, reveling in the magic of the warm day. The leggy stands of late-summer yellow flowers will soon disappear as will my numbered days of leisure.

The arrival of a letter from the administration rings the death knell: the faculty is to convene at school the first week of September.

I feel excited and ready to start yet this enthusiasm is peppered by trepidation because this school year will be different from any I have known in the past.

It seems harmless enough. Two days of staff meetings in the morning, a break for lunch, followed by free time in the afternoon for teachers to meet in departments.

Once I receive the letter, my idyllic vacation ends in my mind.

Day One arrives.

Patrick and I let Beth sleep in as we set out early for the 20-minute commute to school. We have driven the route several times, timing exactly how long it will take to arrive…not too soon and certainly not too late.

A dense fog lays low over the house and the vineyards, giving the impression the only reality that exists is the three feet visible ahead of us. We are engulfed in greyness, an eerie start to our journey.

Our route takes us through two villages. The stores are louvered shut; only the cafés open at this early hour.

Workers in blue and grey overalls are seated or standing at counters enjoying coffee and *tartines,* although we muse some may be nursing more spirited beverages to chase the chill away.

We cross over the bridge spanning the A-6 expressway to Paris. It occurs to me I would love to escape.

But this is it. I am no longer a tourist in France. I am part of the workforce, on the same level with my French colleagues, responsible for teaching English for an entire school year.

Can I do it?

I always took pleasure in preparing my American classroom in August, decorating bulletin boards, printing out ominous pages of classroom rules and grading policies, which hopefully would put the fear of God in the students. Not possible in France. Teachers have no access to the classrooms before the start of school. These two teacher days are all the time we will have to organize our classrooms since vacations are sacrosanct. No one works until the last moment of vacation has ended.

We pass the school to enter the teachers' parking lot, which is located on the far side of the courtyard.

I wear a simple dress and flat shoes, hoping to look professional but not too plain, and certainly not so flashy as to draw attention to myself.

Giving Patrick a peck on the cheek, I exit the car. I take my empty briefcase from the back seat; lacing the two leather straps in my hand gives me a sense of protection.

I cross the courtyard.

Two teachers are walking in front of me about five yards away. I slow down to avoid them but watch where they are going since I do not remember much from my June visit.

I open the left double door of the main building. Between the door and a window is a glass case that encloses a bulletin board for announcements.

On a large white paper is written: "Welcome to *la Rentrée* 1999."

The school still smells of summer, a bit musty from being enclosed over the warm months, with the pungent odor of freshly waxed floors.

The teachers' room is on the left.

In the center of the room are four rows of oblong worktables, flanked by faded wooden and metal chairs. Through the bay of windows on the far wall, teachers can see the students in the courtyard, although on this workday everything is blissfully silent, like the last few minutes before a party when everything is ready, and nothing remains but the expectation of the guests arriving.

Several teachers are standing about, catching up with their colleagues about their summer vacation. Inside jokes, teasing, rapid-fire half-spoken sentences.

I put my purse and briefcase down on a far table, feeling as awkward as a teenager arriving alone at a dance.

Two men are in line at the espresso machine ready to put their coin in the slot for a shot of java to drop down and flow into little orange plastic cups.

Take a breath, Jackie.

No one speaks to me. It is all up to me.

I gingerly approach two women who are at a pause in their conversation. "*Bonjour, Je m'appelle Jackie.*

Je suis l'Américaine."

They know who I am.

I had met a few teachers last spring when visiting Monique, but I do not remember their names.

Mireille, a short woman with a mop of tight black curls and rimless glasses, smiles at me. I decide she is going to be my new best friend. She is the branch I am now clinging to for support.

"Welcome to our little school," she says. The other one, Jeannette, taller, thinner, prettier, with a steely perfect smile, nods in agreement.

Mireille asks how long I have been in France.

She is especially curious about my relationship with Monique.

"How long have you known her?" she asks.

"Do you hear from her often?"

We all have heard in great detail about your beautiful home and your school from Monique," Mireille adds dryly.

Jeannette listens.

I am taken aback at the grilling about Monique.

I sense something is underlying their attitude. There is something reserved, a hesitation, about giving me a full-throttled welcome.

I would later discover the source of their cautious reception.

We are scheduled to start meetings at 9:00. It is 9:20.

A man in his forties, the only one wearing a tie which rests against his pastel no-iron shirt, comes into the room carrying an officious clipboard.

He is the vice-principal.

The teachers give him no welcome.

Monsieur Girard has a round baby face, chocolate brown hair with only a few wisps of grey and a soft, spongy-looking body that betrays a preference for personal indulgence rather than exercise.

He walks up to me, passing by the other teachers, to shake my hand. "Hello, my name is Monsieur Girard," he says in English with a heavy French accent. He sounds like a student rotely reciting from the first page of an English language primer.

The formality of this Frenchman intrigues me.

In the States, the same person would say, "Hello, my name is George Smith." It would seem starchy to hear, "Hello, my name is Mister Smith."

But "Monsieur Girard" he is.

He turns to the group and speaks above the chatter in a loud voice. "*Silence, s'il vous plaît.*"

It takes a moment to get their attention.

"Everyone, this is our new exchange teacher. Have you had time to speak with Madame Donnelly? As you may know, she is the first exchange teacher we have ever had at this school. She will be replacing Madame Aubin, assuming the responsibility for her English classes.

We expect great things of her and hope to learn a lot from her American methods Monique has told us about."

I immediately sense danger. There is nothing more offsetting than a colleague daring to appear superior to the others.

This is my moment to dilute his message.

"*Bonjour,* I am so pleased to be here working with you. I am no expert, simply one eager to learn from you, and I hope you will help me," I quickly respond.

The teachers smile faintly, some offering a word of welcome.

"Let's get moving," Monsieur Monsieur Girard says, opening the door of the faculty room as if to let the animals out of the barn.

CHAPTER 21

Gathering Storm

I FOLLOW MIREILLE AND Jeannette, my new *amies*, crossing the empty courtyard to the community room which is in the cafeteria building.

The chairs are set up theater-style in front of an oblong table.

Monsieur Girard takes his place in front of the chattering group.

The teachers are delighted to see one another again and catch up. They are in no mood to listen to him.

"Attention. Attention. Please let's get started. Quiet please. Quiet."

Clearly, the teachers are not in sync with him or his program.

"Before running through the agenda, I want to welcome you all back. Let's make this year memorable, one of the best ever," Monsieur says, smiling mechanically.

I think to myself in every school at the start of the year, the pep message is always the same.

"Let's go, team. Get in there and do a great job!"

I think of Monique in my school back home. I can see my colleagues grazing at the coffee and donut table catching up with each other after the summer break.

Susan distributes printouts of schedules and class lists. She jokes with the teachers and feels at home with them, a member of the team.

The general meeting will then break up, and the teachers will go to work in their classrooms and have department meetings.

I am confident the teachers Monique met at the party at our house will shepherd her throughout the day.

Monique should be pleased by the *esprit de corps* of the group.

The first four rows in front of Monsieur Girard are empty. The teachers choose to sit in the back, making it obvious they are reluctant participants, and demonstrating a "show me" attitude toward him.

I am introduced. I put my hand up to wave, but I am asked to stand up. I dart up in front of the sea of strangers, nod, and return quickly to the safety of my chair.

The vice-principal talks about policies he wants to implement this year.

One teacher, Bruno, punctuates the administrator's speech with a few choice guffawing remarks, establishing his role as leader of the teacher pack.

Monsieur Girard is not pleased.

The administrator taunts the faculty by announcing our provisional schedules will be distributed on the second workday. We will not learn our schedule and workload until then.

The teachers groan, then explode.

"Why is that? Why the delay? *C'est ridicule!*"

He calmly replies they are still being adjusted.

End of conversation on that topic.

This French school system seems a bit improvised for my taste, and the feeling is shared by my colleagues. Didn't he have all summer to organize everything?

I am anxious to get my schedule, to learn what I will be teaching and when.

Unlike an American high school where teachers work the same

schedule every day of the week, French teachers have varied schedules, which I look forward to. It will relieve the monotony of the American schedule, which never changes.

Another bonus, in France, there are never classes on Wednesday afternoons, which allows the students time to participate in sports.

French teachers earn significantly less money than American counterparts, but commensurate to their student contact hours, it is somewhat understandable.

We spend the balance of the morning listening to Monsieur Girard talk about modest renovations to the facility, future teacher meetings, and expectations for students. Few pay attention.

There is a small, round-shouldered woman sitting in the back who walks to the front when summoned.

I recognize her as the principal, Madame Laubert. She takes her place to the left of Monsieur Girard.

"Welcome staff," she says, in a weak, modulated voice. I hope you enjoy your year and have many successes."

That's it. Short and sweet. Madame returns to the back of the room.

Monsieur Girard takes back the reins and continues with his agenda.

We break for lunch.

Bruno approaches me. "Welcome, Madame."

"Please call me Jackie."

"Jackie, will you join us for lunch? We are going out to a small *resto* not far from school. You can ride with me."

I immediately like Bruno. His golden-brown Middle Eastern face, deep brown eyes, and deep velvet voice remind me of Yul Brynner.

He wears, what I will learn later, is his uniform: a brown khaki jacket over a T-shirt and jeans.

This is an incredibly kind gesture, as I would have been at a loss to what to do for lunch.

Initially, the teachers seem to be distant toward me. I assume it is because I am new. They use the *vous* form, which means *you.*

One uses the *vous* form with strangers, or to show respect. It is formal and reserved, rather than the cozy, cushy *tu* form, which also means *you* and is used with colleagues, friends and family.

Within minutes of our meeting, Bruno speaks to me as *tu,* warming my heart, tantamount to a verbal hug. The other teachers follow suit.

Mireille, and Jeannette, the tall Scottish English teacher I had met in the lounge, and I pile into Bruno's VW, moving papers, old coffee cups, and a briefcase aside to make room. The car reeks of French cigarettes.

We drive for ten minutes to the restaurant, which resembles a Bavarian lodge. The interior is dark; the stained glass windows are not of saints in pious poses but of flowers encircling glasses of different ales and wines.

We join the other teachers sitting at long banquet tables. The restaurant has the stale scent of cigarettes and beer.

The waiters bob in between us, taking our orders, talking above the loud, laughing diners.

Oh, I am going to make it, I think. *This is really fun.*

Jeannette is a vegetarian. I order a meatless entrée to bond with her. While my colleagues choose mouthwatering *steak-frites,* or Alsatian sausage and sauerkraut, I content myself with a salad and celery soup soaking up the last remnants with the French bread.

We each order a glass of wine to complement our meal.

This is my opportunity to observe the teachers. They are casually dressed, quite relaxed, still in fine form after the summer break. There is a palpable affection for each other, which I sensed in the teachers' meeting and is confirmed at lunch. However, later I will learn, they feel under attack like soldiers in the trenches, which explains the tension in the faculty meeting.

We are to report back at 1:30. We have not been served at 1:00 p.m. I start to get uneasy like I am going to get a tardy on my first day.

"Bruno, will this be a problem if we are not back on time?"

He smiles. "I will call."

Bruno takes his miniature portable phone from his breast pocket to speed-dial the school.

"Please tell Monsieur Girard we will be late."

CHAPTER 22

Showtime!
The First Day of Classes

I FELT LIKE A pro arriving at school for the second day of meetings, having mastered how to buy meal tickets, and where all of the bathrooms are located.

I go directly to the teachers' lounge, where I see some familiar faces.

Jeannette and Mireille are talking near the window.

"*Bonjour*," I say as I approach them.

Jeannette responds in English, "Oh, Jackie, good morning. Big day today - we are getting our provisional schedules and class lists to see which darlings we are going to teach."

"Have you heard from Monique?" asks Mireille.

"I heard from her briefly that she likes the school and the students. She has been teaching for a week now and seems to be fine."

Monsieur Girard enters the lounge.

He is all business and devoid of any chit chat.

"Please go directly to the meeting room so we can begin on time."

Bruno asks how long this meeting will last. He is clearly not pleased with the vice-principal's delay in distributing the schedules.

Monsieur Girard has a healthy respect for Bruno, who is our alpha: the only person who can stand up to him.

"I think we could be done quickly if we all leave now," Monsieur Girard replies.

We receive our schedules and class lists. Those teaching the same subjects compare class lists and are dumbfounded to see one class has seven students and another an overload of 32.

"What's this about?" they ask Monsieur Girard.

He smiles, slyly. "Don't worry, this will all be worked out soon."

We break for departmental meetings.

I meet Viviane, the fourth member of the English department. She is pleasant but reserved. I think, unlike Mireille and Jeannette, she will take some time to warm up to me.

Viviane takes the lead in the meeting, outlining the teaching outcomes we want to achieve this year: a firm foundation in English grammar and basic fluency.

The discussion turns to discipline. My new colleagues complain about student behavior and the lack of support by Madame Tabata, the sexy disciplinarian.

"You never know what kind of response you are going to get from her."

I am asked what we do in my American school about unruly students.

I feel cornered by the question.

I dodge, saying we have a set system of discipline, but it is not perfect.

My mind is racing. I wonder what it is about "student behavior" they are referring to. The students seemed so well-behaved to me last June. And despite Monique's cryptic allusions to *naughty* students, I thought she was exaggerating as she tends to be a bit negative.

I have never taught middle school, but I am confident it could not be that much different than teaching my high school students. Perhaps they are a bit more unruly because of their age?

Then I remember how I was in seventh grade and am afraid…

Still, I am eager for my year teaching to begin and can't wait to get into my classroom.

My classroom is on the second floor of the main building. I turn the key and peer into the room. I remember from my June visit, there are four rows of oblong tables, each allowing two students to sit side by side. The chairs are stacked on the tables, as they will be at the close of every day to allow the cleaning staff to sweep.

Before I left the States, I feared I would not learn the students' names quickly, so I have brought little cardboard tents with red and blue borders, which, together with the white background, represent the colors of the French and American flags. Darling and very useful.

They are like place cards at a formal dinner but larger. I will write out the name of each student on a card that will be placed in front of them, so I can connect the name and face at the same time.

I organize these name cards by class and secure with a rubber band. I will distribute them first thing tomorrow morning in class.

In the drawer of my desk, I put pens, erasers, and chalk.

Who can resist me? I am so ready to start teaching. And I am so excited!

I tack photos of regions of the United States on the bulletin board.

All set!

The following day Patrick drives me to school. I feel like a student on the first day of school, nervous and apprehensive.

With a peck on his cheek, I leave him to begin the first day.

The teachers are milling around in the lounge, telling stories, and laughing among themselves.

Mireille sees me and shouts across the room, "Hey, Jackie. This is the big day! *Bon courage!*"

Others chime in, "Let us know if you need anything."

The first class is at 8:00 a.m.

The prison-type bell clangs loudly.

Mireille and I leave the lounge to go into the courtyard, where the students are scurrying to line up in their assigned areas by class.

I straighten my back and summon my courage as I approach my students, who are loosely assembled in a line.

"Good morning," I say to them in English. "Good morning," they chant back.

Many students laugh nervously. They do not know who I am, as I am not a familiar face.

I lead them upstairs to my classroom.

So far, so good.

They push to get to a seat near their friends, pull the chairs down with a clang, each one seemingly at a different time.

I again say, "Good morning."

I call each student up to the front to receive their name card.

"Pierre Dulain"

"Margot Lebrun"

Each student rises to receive his or her card.

So far, so good. Oh, this is going to be just fine.

I turn my back to write "Welcome!" on the board. The students take this opportunity to exchange cards with each other, so I no longer have a prayer of learning their names. I should have known these are not like my placid high school students, who are always too tired in the morning to act out.

And then we begin.

I distribute stapled copies of the first lesson taken from the English book since the textbooks will not be distributed until later in the week.

"Quiet, please."

"Please turn to page one."

"Who would like to read?" I ask in English.

Silence.

I don't know if they did not understand or are too reticent to participate.

I ask the most alert student to read.

He squirms a bit, clears his throat, and begins.

As he reads, I realize I have no idea what he is saying, since his heavily French-accented English is unintelligible.

Got to work on that.

Pointing to a smiling girl, I say, "Please continue."

As she reads, a student in the back throws an eraser at his friend to get his attention.

The young girl soldiers on.

"Stop that. That is enough," I chide the boy interrupting her.

I ask a basic question about the reading.

Students say out of turn,

"I don't understand you."

"What did you just say?"

"Oh, Robert, you are so dumb."

"No, I am not, you are dumb."

"Yeah, thanks a lot."

This scene, minus, of course, the now-abandoned name cards, plays out in all of the other classes. To my great relief, some classes work out better than others, but in each it is a struggle.

I am sure it will get better. This is just the first day.

Patrick is waiting for me in the parking lot at the end of the day.

He is seated in the car, peacefully reading a book.

I walk slowly to the car.

I am exhausted.

My mind is mulling over my day.

"How did it go?" he asks cheerfully.

I peer in the car at his smiling face.

I know his day has been delightful: shopping, reading, and a bit of television.

Perhaps he took a nap?

I get in the car, collapse back into my seat, and stare straight ahead.

"Done with Day One. Let's go home."

CHAPTER 23

To Arcachon and Beyond

Before Friday classes of the second week, Monsieur Girard meets with the faculty to announce the provisional schedule we have been working under will change.

He is a man who does not tax himself greatly about doing his job well. In fact, both the first and second iterations of the schedule give us drastically unequal class loads, apparently for no reason.

This is clearly not his concern. Is he careless or passive-aggressive? Why does he allow this to happen?

The faculty is understandably upset with the haphazard scheduling.

Madame Laubert took no role in the planning and, through her weakness and tendency to hide in her bunker of an office, seems unaware of his actions.

The reaction of the faculty to the lack of planning simmers but has not yet reached a boil.

Any efforts to get him to rectify the scheduling appears fruitless.

In my case, my new schedule not only changes the days and hours of my classes, but in one case, even re-assigns a section of my students to another teacher.

It is difficult for any teacher to leave a class and break in a new group after the year has begun, and equally hard on the students, but Monsieur Girard does not seem to be concerned about that either.

Because I am going to teach a new group of students on Monday, I must meet with my current class to announce the schedule change today.

Before starting the lesson, I make the announcement.

"Students, there has been a change in your program. You will report to room 33 on Monday for English class. This will be our last time together."

What I think is a public service announcement detonates a bomb.

The students become very agitated and angry.

"This is not fair."

"Why is it always us?"

"Who is going to teach us?"

For forty minutes, they shout their displeasure, drop books on the floor in protest, and accuse me of having something to do with the change.

I would like to think that even after this short amount of time, their affection for me makes them unhappy about the switch, but I sense it runs deeper than that.

There is nothing I can do. It is impossible to talk over the din to explain anything.

I feel like I am trapped in a cage with wild animals. I am stunned at their reaction.

I try my best to calm them, but they cannot be appeased.

I stand behind my desk, helpless as they act out their anger.

I can only watch the clock move slowly to the end of the hour.

The bell rings.

The students storm out of class.

I sit down at my desk, stunned. I cannot move.

In all my years of teaching, I have never seen such rage in young people.

This is only early September. How am I going to make it?

I straighten the books on my desk to assert some control in my life, gather my purse and exit the school.

As I leave the shadows of the building, I feel the warm bake of the sun on my face.

Even though it is September, it still feels like summer, although the angle of the afternoon sun is decidedly different.

Beth and Patrick are in the car waiting to take me to spend our afternoon in Arcachon, a beautiful Atlantic seaside resort, just a little more than an hour away.

Beth is in the front seat wearing sunglasses, a sleeveless shirt, and shorts. She is savoring the last few days of vacation before she leaves for college, still in summer mode.

I get into the back seat.

As we drive, I lean forward to describe the horrific hour I have just spent with this class.

"You just wouldn't believe it. I couldn't do anything to calm them. What kind of a culture is this? They were literally out of their minds with anger."

"Mom, don't worry. These kids aren't your students anymore. It will all work out."

As we approach the coast, we watch the scenery change from vineyards to pine forests and soft undulating sand dunes.

We park the car near the beach. I am soothed by the salt smell of the ocean, the rhythmic roll of waves thundering to shore, the dance of white caps on the cobalt blue of the water.

I want to pretend I am still on vacation far away from St. Pierre.

Only a few people walk in the sand, holding sunhats in their hands as the wind blows them along.

Just a few weeks ago, this beach was crowded with August vacationers filling up the cafés that lined the boardwalk or napping under blue beach umbrellas.

Where are they now?

The footsteps of children who used to run in the sand to the water have been swept away. Now only memories of these summer vacationers remain like ghosts on this sunny fall day.

The restaurant we choose seems to still smell of suntan cream. Decorative fishermen nets drape the walls; starfish and various crustaceans are perched in windows.

The cover of the menu sports a crusty old fisherman's face with a corncob pipe perched in his mouth, winking at us.

Beth and Patrick think this is going to be a grand afternoon of seaside and seafood.

Beth orders a *salade de crudités* and crab legs. Patrick cannot resist the fresh deep-fried calamari and fries accompanied by a tall blond Kronenbourg 1664 in a frosted glass.

I cannot order. I cannot eat. I console myself with a glass of wine, which slips easily down my throat as they enjoy their meal. I order another.

I feel like someone who has seen a terrible accident and cannot communicate the horror of it to passersby.

This should be a beautiful moment in my life, being on the Atlantic, in France, with my husband and daughter. Instead, I am overcome with fear that I have put myself in an impossible position; that through a colossal, arrogant misjudgment of my skill and experience, I am destined to spend an endless school year in hell.

I am a fool.

How could a dream crumble so fast?

En route back to the house, I lie in the backseat of the car in a fetal position, eyes closed, trying to sort out what I can do. Neither Patrick nor Beth can help me.

The car jolts as we approach a roundabout where others are entering the circle from different roads.

I lift my head and see a car approach us, fast. It could ram us.

I think *O.K. hit me. Please do. Just break my leg so I can go home again.*

The car spins past us and away.

I experience sheer disappointment.

It is the closest I have ever felt to being suicidal or craved being maimed as the perfect solution to a problem.

CHAPTER 24

The Big Reveal

Morning in the teachers' lounge is the time when colleagues chat with one another, get that last cup of coffee, check their mail, and read the announcements which are posted on a large whiteboard next to the windows.

I find Jeannette always has a moment for me. Since she also teaches English, her advice is pertinent and helpful. She decodes for me what the daily announcements mean since they are written in a shorthand of initials and abbreviations.

Bruno makes a brief guest appearance to say *bonjour* to everyone, then retires to the smokers' lounge.

His friendship and support are important to me, so on many mornings, I endanger my healthy lungs just to spend some time with him.

I admire him. He is a take-charge guy: students have no choice but to fall into line.

The time spent chatting with him is worth the reek of smoke on my clothes.

Overall, I feel like I am making inroads with the staff, but with some, I sense there is something keeping me from winning them over.

One day at lunch, I discover what it is.

I find Jeannette and Bruno at a table with a few other colleagues. They invite me to join them. We talk about our two schools' systems, salaries, discipline and, of course, vacations.

Jeannette asks me if I ever taught French at the university level.

Bruno answers that he remembers, from my letter, I had.

"What letter, Bruno?" I ask.

"Oh, the one you had arranged to be placed in all of our mailboxes last June."

I have absolutely no idea what he is talking about.

"What did the letter look like?"

Bruno answers, "It was a long letter, explaining why you would be an excellent asset to our school, outlining your successes and honors. It was very impressive," he says, his voice trailing.

It suddenly becomes clear to me.

That had to be the application letter I wrote to be accepted into the Exchange Program. It was loaded with impressive details about my professional experience. It was meant to be shared with the evaluation committee and then sent on to my French school. Never, never, to be shared with anyone else.

Delving further, Bruno suspects it was Monique who had asked Madame Laubert for the letter, duplicated it, and put it in everyone's mailbox since she is the only teacher who has the principal's ear.

If she had indeed done this, be she maladroit or spiteful, she got the desired effect.

Before meeting me in the fall, the teachers must have thought I was overbearing and too sure of my own worth since I evidently felt a need to give them a letter telling them how wonderful I was.

"Bruno, please believe I never asked Monique to do that."

Bruno smiles.

"I believe you, Jackie. This is just exactly something Monique would do."

Bruno adds that Monique, after her visit to the American school, bragged about the extensive teaching materials, computers, and school facility she was going to enjoy. She made it clear she was more than happy to leave her French colleagues and school for a better one.

Jeannette added, "Not content with that, she told us, 'Wait until this American teacher comes here. She will show you what education is all about.'"

With a remark like that, I could not have been better set up to fail.

I see why it is taking time for many of them to overcome their mistrust of me.

Now, with Bruno's support, he will make it clear to the others that the letter did not come from me but from Monique.

I wrestle in my mind why she would do that to me.

CHAPTER 25

Strike One

AFTER THE FIRST FEW weeks of school, I am settling into a pattern where I know my students' work, can navigate around campus and am winning over the faculty by dint of my persistence.

The students continue to be challenging, and I often find myself praying to get through the day. There are, however, some days classes run reasonably well. I just never know how my day is going to go.

Patrick drives me to school on Monday morning on what I hoped would be a good day.

I make a dash to the teachers' room to get my record book from my locker when I notice a lot of commotion in the lounge. The teachers who are usually busy getting ready for their day are talking in groups.

They are unusually animated.

I look for Laurence. I have come to rely on her for guidance. She is a kind, gentle colleague who teaches French at the school. Laurence is not only an excellent educator but serves on the faculty advisory board and is a member of the parent-teachers' association.

She is always in the know.

Laurence is conferring with Bruno in the corner of the lounge. I sense this is a power pow-wow. She sees me and beckons me to join them.

"I am sorry to tell you this, Jackie, but we are on strike. There will be no classes today or until further notice."

Laurence adds, "I realize you are in an awkward position since you are a visiting teacher here, but our faculty has taken a vote to strike. We are not going to have classes."

My chest gets tight. I am so confused... I did not see this coming.

"What is going on? Why a strike? Did I miss something here?"

"Jackie, *calme-toi*. We are protesting the class numbers. Monsieur Girard is totally unresponsive to us. We have tried talking to him about it, and nothing has been resolved.

For the students' sake, we cannot accept this situation.

We must strike."

Many teachers think there are underlying issues beyond the schedule and class numbers.

Monsieur Girard is an ambitious man. A strike will be reported to the Educational Administration of Bordeaux. Madame Laubert will take the fall since this is under her tutelage.

Who could benefit? Who would be placed in charge when she is gone? It is obvious.

I need to add that, in my opinion, for the French, going on strike is a national tradition.

It is in the DNA of French people to resist and revolt. The spirit of the French Revolution seems to play out in many ways in their everyday life.

Subway, bus, and taxi strikes are common occurrences. The Louvre can be open in the morning and closed in the afternoon by a strike. It is the way it is.

"What should I do?" I ask.

Laurence counsels, "Do what you think is best, but I would suggest you abstain from all votes and not go to class."

I trust Laurence, and I want to be part of the effort even if I find it stressful.

The students are outside, milling around the courtyard, waiting for the opening bell, unaware this day will not be normal. I can see them through the window, jostling each other, pushing, or gossiping in groups.

They think it is business as usual.

In the past, I have participated in teacher strikes in the United States which are well-organized, announced in advance, and equally upsetting. They are euphemistically called "job actions" and are usually the result of failed contract negotiations to protect health care benefits and to pressure the administration to give across-the-board raises. When a strike is announced, everything shuts down.

But in this case, the French school remains open, and the teachers and staff have to monitor the students whose parents send them to school.

The teachers who would typically have class first hour are instructed to go outside to the courtyard, line their students up, and wait.

Bruno walks to the middle of the courtyard.

In his strong, deep voice, he announces there will be no classes because the teachers are on strike.

Students' reactions are mixed: delighted, stunned, or aggressive.

"What is going on? When did this happen?" they ask.

Others, naturally, are elated and scream, *Bravo! Pas de classes!*

Since I have class first hour, I join my colleagues who must stay outdoors to watch the kids who did not return home.

It is like doing time in a prison yard.

To be honest, for me, it is a welcome reprieve from facing students across my desk because, at least here in the courtyard, I know what I am doing.

St. Pierre is a public middle school that draws its students from middle to lower class families; some are gypsies, many parents are unemployed.

At first, just a few of my students shyly approach me. Then more students, many I do not teach, encircle me.

They are curious about this American creature who is teaching at their school.

"Where do you come from?"

"What is your favorite music?"

"Do you eat hamburgers every day?"

"Are all Americans rich?

The young faces of these French children are fresh and so impressionable.

Most students have never seen an American. I feel like an exotic bird and am deeply conscious of the image I must portray so my country will be seen in a good light. In fact, this moral charge to represent America well is my dominant thought through every moment of the school year.

In every interaction I have, be it at school, in a store, or on the street, since I am the only foreigner in the area, I feel I am "the other", the different one, which weighs heavily on me.

Day two of the strike, the teachers meet in the lounge at lunchtime while the students are in the cafeteria.

Laurence is on the strike team. She is chosen to update us on the current status of the negotiations, the support we have from the parents, and how the resistance is going to play out.

"We will continue to monitor the students in the courtyard during our regular hours of class.

Before you leave, the Strike Committee wants to take an official vote to show faculty support for this strike."

The roll call is read in alphabetical order. When my name is called, I answer, *je m'abstiens.* My colleagues look at me. Laurence quickly explains, "By her teacher contract, Jackie does not have the right to participate in any political activity here in France, but she supports us in spirit."

The teachers express approval. They understand.

The strike vote is carried by a wide majority.

We break for lunch.

We continue to discuss the strike as we eat.

"How long do you think the strike will last?" I ask Laurence, feeling totally adrift in a system I am trying to understand.

"We will see, perhaps a week or longer," she replies.

Laurence quips, "Welcome to *L'Education Nationale*, Jackie. This is how things are run around here."

Although I like the break and the chance to meet the students informally and learn what they are interested in, and I do want to support my colleagues, this is not a good situation.

I have just gotten up a head of steam in class, started to get to know the students personally and understand the class dynamic, and am working out how to write lesson plans that work well for them.

This interruption destroys the momentum we were building; now we will have to start all over again, as if from Day One.

CHAPTER 26

What's a Strike Without *Pâté?*

BY NOW, OUR TEACHER strike is in the fourth day.

The morning passes slowly as we monitor the students outside.

The balmy autumn weather takes a turn for the worse as if reflecting the gloom and stress we are feeling. Today is cold, with a slight drizzle.

After two hours of walking about, it is time for the morning break. The monitors, young professionals whose job it is to track students and enforce after-school detention, take over in the court-yard.

I find Laurence, who has just left the administration building.

"How goes it with you?" I ask.

"Not well for the moment. Monsieur Girard, with the complicity of Madame Laubert, is still apart from us on finding a solution. This might take a few more days."

We walk to the teachers' room together for a cup of espresso to warm our fingers.

I sense something is different.

My colleagues are clustered around an oblong table in the center of the room.

I work my way into the group to find an unbelievable spread of homemade food they have brought to work.

It is a fellowship meal.

On the worktables, now transformed into an incredible buffet, the organizers have placed terrines of *pâté,* accompanied by bottles of kitchen-made sweet wine.

There are also selections of Bordeaux reds and whites, cornichon pickles, trays of hams, salami, and veal, baguettes of French bread, as well as thick slices of wheat bread, and cold scalloped potatoes. We picnic on paper plates.

Small white plastic cups serve as wine or water glasses.

Although it is not noon, we all mill about sampling the fare.

"Who brought this great *pâté*? Jean-Paul? You have outdone yourself!"

And the farm-to-table regional food far exceeds the chips and cheese and pastries I might have provided.

Bruno taps on a glass jar to get our attention.

"*Attention, s'il vous plaît.*"

"The negotiating team would like to update you on our progress or lack of it. It is truly frustrating getting the administration to own this problem and work with us for a solution. The unequal distribution of students is but one issue. There are extenuating personnel issues as well we will share with you later.

We must act as a team.

For this reason, we are going to call for another vote to decide jointly if we return to work. We have not gotten anywhere close to where we need to be. I suggest we keep the pressure on and continue the strike."

Not all teachers are of one mind about not returning to class.

Questions are volleyed to him about other aspects of the strike. I barely have a clue what is going on, although, being a faculty member, I am deeply implicated in it.

Bruno calls for the vote.

Majority rules.

The strike will continue until further notice.

Thank God the Exchange Program forbids me from participating in the political issues of our school.

We go back to the courtyard for the afternoon patrol.

The next day we meet again at 12:00 for an update.

The president of the French Parent Teacher Association is present to talk with us.

To my surprise, the parent representatives state that overall, the parents polled support the strike even though they are inconvenienced by having their children's routine interrupted.

The following Monday, during our update meeting, Madame Laubert comes to the faculty room to talk to us. She explains in a soft, unsure voice she was not aware of the skewed class lists as it is the vice principal's job, and she is confident the problem of class sizes will be resolved.

Bruno shakes his head in anger, quickly stands up, and approaches Madame Laubert.

He wags his finger in her face, accuses her of being totally incompetent, and insists she should resign.

His booming baritone voice vibrates every piece of furniture.

I slip to the floor and, literally, crawl under a nearby table, as if I am under a barrage attack. I put my head in my hands and hide unnoticed.

This is insanity. How can I stay here? I have never seen this kind of outburst among professionals.

Madame Laubert leaves.

The strike will continue into the second week.

I am starting to get used to walking in circles in the courtyard, talking to students. It is mindless and stress-free, unlike teaching.

In the meantime, Monique has gotten word about the strike from one of her nameless faculty informants.

She is furious.

I receive a terse phone call.

"Jackie, I expect you to not participate in the strike. You should go to class and work.

If you participate, then I will be docked pay. Don't do it."

I am surprised she does not feel solidarity with her colleagues.

Her reaction is upsetting; this is an ambush out of the blue.

I seek out Laurence and Bruno to talk about her phone call.

They are annoyed at her reaction and the obvious lack of *esprit de corps*.

"Jackie, don't worry. You have no choice. You are doing the right thing by not opposing us."

How ironic it is, Bruno adds, that the previous year, when Monique was unfairly accused of striking a child, the faculty went on strike on her behalf.

"She owes us this support even at a distance," he says.

Laurence adds it also is not certain she will lose money.

Not wanting to provoke her further, I do not respond to Monique.

As quickly as the strike starts, it ends.

The following Monday, a sign posted in the entry announces the strike is over, and classes will resume immediately.

CHAPTER 27

Class Struggle

THE SCHOOL BELL RINGS.

I gather my students who are lined up in their assigned area, and accompany them to our classroom.

The students push their way into the room, jostling each other, banging into the rectangular desks.

The students lower the chairs stacked on the table with such force that some unoccupied chairs topple over and are not picked up immediately.

They obviously find this abrupt return to class unsettling.

"Sit down, please. We will begin."

Not only can they not hear my voice above the din, but they are in no mindset to comply, even if they could.

They demand to know what is happening.

I feel like I am on a tennis court returning balls hit by 20 different players as they fire questions to me.

"What's going on?" "How come the strike is over?"

"I'm not certain, but I will let you know," I reply.

"Now, let's begin." After the hiatus, I struggle to remember all of their names.

The story we are working on is about a girl named Mary, who wants to go grocery shopping. She is looking for ingredients to make a cake.

The story is not exciting, but since the lesson introduces food vocabulary in English, it has some value.

I read aloud the three-paragraph story we read almost two weeks ago, and most have certainly forgotten.

I call on a student whom I remember is quite serious, asking him the first prepared question.

"René, what does Mary do after school?"

He begins to answer, but his words are drowned out by the smart alecks in the class who shout in French,

"I couldn't care less." or "She is a loser, anyway."

I turn to write his answer on the board for the class to copy.

"Is that an I or an L?" "I can't read your writing," they call out, almost in unison.

They are right. My Palmer Method handwriting is different than French script.

I resort to printing. The tap, tap, tap of the chalk gives a sense of order.

"Copy this down," I say firmly.

"I don't have a pen." "I need some *Blanco;* I made a mistake."

Blanco is part of the students' tool kit. It is the French version of "White-Out" used when one makes a mistake. My students in the States would have been happy to cross out or write over the word. These students have been trained to be tidy.

My white chalk breaks under the pressure of my printing, snapping into shards. I pick up another piece of chalk on the ledge. It is red.

"Should we change our pen from blue to red?" they ask.

I turn away and take a breath. *So, this is middle school!*

I am as far from my cooperative high school students as I can possibly be, and I still have 30 minutes left of class.

The few motivated students complete the writing assignment

while I silence the others, who amuse themselves by dropping their notebooks, or hitting their neighbor.

Twenty more minutes.

We continue to talk about Mary in the supermarket.

The textbook is British, so the terms do not align with American English.

"Mary pushes her trolley down the aisle."

One student volunteers to reread the first paragraph.

The student's reading is labored, but he gets through it.

Ten more minutes.

To veer from the story and personalize the lesson, I ask, "What do you like to eat?" As the students shout out their favorites, I make a list on the board which some copy.

"For your homework, write 'I like….' listing the foods you like to eat."

That should be easy enough.

The bell rings; the students barge out, except for René, who lags behind.

"Madame, I really like English. I want to learn how to speak it."

I look at his big sincere eyes.

I vow, somehow, he is going to learn English, despite the chaos in his class.

CHAPTER 28

A Trip to Paris

THE INTERNATIONAL EXCHANGE ORGANIZATION requires that we attend meetings in Paris in late September. The idea of getting away to Paris is very appealing, though I wonder why we are convening so early in the school year instead of waiting until October or November.

After a few weeks of teaching at St. Pierre, I realize the Exchange Program understands the adjustment period at the very beginning of the year is potentially the most difficult, and the administrators want to resolve any issues we might have before they escalate.

Patrick is finishing up his sojourn in the States. He will meet me in Paris for the meetings.

This gathering is a really big deal in the eyes of Madame Laubert. Very few French teachers penetrate the inner halls of the *Education Nationale* offices, a source of policy, procedures, and major irritations to the French teachers working in the field. The International Exchange Program is prestigious not only in the United States but in France, which is why we are receiving this special attention.

I fly to Paris on Friday and stay with Joëlle for the weekend, before the two-day meetings on Monday and Tuesday.

Joëlle meets me at *Aéroport Charles de Gaulle*. It is like old times.

"How was your trip?" Without waiting for an answer, she continues. "There are three exhibits I think you will like. We can go tomorrow and hit all three if we hustle."

Business as usual.

Joëlle loves art but thinks visiting a museum is a speed contest. We always fly through exhibitions, stopping only at the key pieces noted in our guides.

On Saturday, we go directly to *La Gare d'Orsay* and two art galleries on the Left Bank.

The weather is superb. The chestnut trees are turning color, their leaves floating down, spinning, dancing their way to the sidewalk. It is classic Paris in the fall.

That evening we spend hours at dinner, catching up and talking about life as we have done on previous visits when my life was much simpler.

Joëlle is a dear friend despite the physical distance and cultural differences separating us.

I recount what it is like teaching at St. Pierre and go into detail about the strike and the challenging students I have been assigned.

Being a physician, she can detect depression at a glance.

"Jaaakey, it can't be that bad. We French know our system has flaws, but are you sure these students are really this difficult to handle?"

After four or five more anecdotes of students acting out in class, Joëlle is coming around to my reality.

"*Bof*, it is true our schools aren't what they were. *Courage.*

Maybe in these meetings, you will get some advice."

"And maybe you are right," I say, but I cannot imagine what could solve or salve the problem.

Still, I feel so safe in her apartment.

Sunday in Joëlle's *quartier*, which is on the edge of Paris, is like Sunday in many small towns around the world.

The pace of life slows. Before the midday meal, we have a quick walk to the market to get fresh bread. "Not from here, no, from there, because it is fresher."

If one is fortunate to dine on Sunday in a French family, the meal begins around 1:00. There is a little tune-up of olives, radishes, and cashews, complemented by a liqueur or concentrated fruit nectar.

À table!

The meal smells like home. Often it is oven-roasted chicken with fine herbs, overcooked green beans, crispy golden oven potatoes, followed by a cheese plate, and of course, *tarte aux pommes* or ice cream for dessert. Conversation, like the wine, flows freely.

A digestive nap would be delightful, but my super-kinetic friend suggests we take a nature walk along the Seine.

Tourist boats pass under the bridges as we walk from the right bank to the Île de la Cité, the cradle of Paris.

Having studied French history, I can imagine at every corner the early Celtic fishermen who lived on the island darning their nets or see in my mind the ruins of Roman houses and marketplaces lying beneath our feet.

Looking across the river at *la Conciergerie,* I picture Marie-Antoinette languishing in her cell before being dragged off to her death at the guillotine. Is that the shadow of Quasimodo peering down from the bell towers of *Notre Dame?*

A walk in Paris is a party in my mind.

Of course, in present-day time, it would be a shame not to taste *Bertillon's Bombe Glacées* on *Rue Saint Louis* before returning to Joëlle's apartment.

Monday, I take the *Métro* across the Seine river toward the Eiffel Tower.

The first day meetings are held at the Exchange's educational center on the left bank; the second day, our meeting will be held at the prestigious office of the *Ministère de l'Education Nationale.*

Over coffee, I meet my fellow Exchange teachers. We automatically feel a kinship since we are all on the same adventure: living and working in France. We share our stories.

One man, who is a middle school teacher in the States, teaches the same age level in Nice. His school is not far from the beach, and he has been swimming every day after classes. Score!

Another, a woman, is assigned to the highly competitive, *Lycée Louis-le-Grand,* a high school which prepares the elite students of France to attend the most prestigious colleges. Famous writers, leaders of the French Revolution, political greats, even St Francis de Sales, attended this school. She has an apartment on *Rue Mouffetard,* one of the most highly sought-after places to live on the Left Bank. Her lodging overlooks the narrow medieval street dotted with open-air markets and small smoky cafés. I admit to being quite jealous of the assignment.

I learn from the director I was assigned the St. Pierre school because I have a house large enough to accommodate Monique and her family, not necessarily because it was the best match for me.

Perhaps I too could have lived in Paris were it not for the lodging issue.

In talking with my counterparts, I sense no one feels overwhelmed by their assignment. They like their schools, and the students are manageable. No one has gone on strike or has administrative conflicts in their school.

I am too proud to reveal I do not feel up to the job. That my students are, as Monique described them, "naughty."

Our meetings deal with the mechanics of living in France: when to get your health check for your visa, issues in banking, and receiving a salary abroad.

I pull aside the organizer of the meeting, a young American woman married to a French man, to confide that my school is a challenge. That many of the students assigned to me should be in Special Education or would benefit from psychological counseling, both services not offered in this French school. Her response was assuring.

"Do the best you can. If at some point it is too much, we can work something out." This translates to sending me home. Can't do that: I am too proud to fail.

That evening we are fêted at the residence of the American Ambassador to France, 41 *Rue du Faubourg-Saint-Honoré*, one of the best addresses in Paris, built in 1839 and later the princely home of the Rothschilds.

We are dazzled by the opulence of the architecture and décor as we are escorted to the garden for cocktails and appetizers by elegantly dressed attendants.

Returning to Joëlle's apartment, another delightful evening of good food and conversation.

The following day we meet at the French national education office, the *Ministère de l'Education Nationale*. The French Director of English Studies for France addresses us.

I don't remember much of her talk, except she states it is the quality of what we teach, not the chapters we cover that counts. That reminds me of the dictum of Montaigne that a mind should be

Bien faite, not *bien pleine*: well-formed, not stuffed with information.

That sounds reasonable and assuring.

She also emphasizes that students are to keep lovely notebooks written in a round hand, which will be shared with their parents.

Uh-Oh. Because the students cannot read my handwriting, I have been typing out their lessons, which they glue onto pages in their workbooks. If a beautiful notebook is the by-product of excellent French education, I am in trouble.

Patrick joins me that evening for the last dinner with Joëlle before we depart for Bordeaux the following morning.

I plan to keep in touch with the American teachers I met. Perhaps they will have some good advice for me as the year goes on.

CHAPTER 29

Maybe This Was a Mistake

RETURNING BACK TO SCHOOL, I find my colleagues are curious about the Paris sessions and my reaction to the meetings at the *l'Education Nationale*.

As I return home, I see Diane and Alex are home. Their children are in the gravel driveway kicking the soccer ball to each other. The kids give me a big smile and wave before returning to their game.

I settle in the house, put my work on my desk, give Patrick a kiss on the cheek before going over to see them.

Diane always greets me as if it has been a long time. "Oh, you must come in and see the new table I found."

Would you like a cup of coffee? You look tired." She has become a neighbor and almost a sister to me.

I love being with her.

"Diane, where do you go to get your hair done? I am getting a bit grey and would like to cover it up."

If I were at home in the States, I would have my beauty support team on speed dial. Diane, being younger, colors her hair for fun. In the short time I have known her, she has had auburn, blond, or streaked tresses.

I knew she would know.

"I'm going to get my hair done tomorrow afternoon, as a matter of fact. I can make an appointment for you, too, if you like."

I trust her since Diane is the guru about everything in the area.

This sounds like a great diversion, a girlfriend outing. I am all in.

The following day, I leave with her for the mall.

I imagine, like in Paris, I will find a national chain of salons with beautiful names like *Jean Louis David*, or *Jacques Dessange*.

After all, this is France, the epicenter of beauty and fashion.

The mall is a sprawling single-story complex. The anchor store is a large hypermarket selling groceries, household items, clothing, and car parts.

The retail shops are accessible through various entrances.

We serpentine our way through the corridors, turning left, then right, then right again until we reach the little salon at the end of a series of stores.

The salon is not a national franchise but an independently owned business.

The décor of the salon is black and grey chic. The reception area is lined with enormous posters of pouting glassy-eyed models sporting hairdos one does not see in the street.

Inside the inner sanctum are rows of sinks and chairs.

There are women in all stages of repair. Some are getting a shampoo, others are tin-foiled, or have their hair covered in goop.

A few stylists are snipping and gossiping as the locks of hair fall from the black capes to the floor.

My stylist greets me and leads me to her station. On the counter, framed pictures of her children are interspersed with spray bottles and potions.

"What would you like today? A cut? A trim? A color?"

My daily French is pretty good, but I find I am lacking in beauty terms. I stumble. I end up telling her I would like her to decide what color would work for me.

After all, I am in France.

She disappears to mix the ingredients that will make me beautiful.

She returns with a round bowl and a wide brush. Dividing my hair into sections, she slaps the color on my hair.

I try to read a fashion magazine but eventually remove my glasses so she can color the sides of my head.

I give in to fatigue and close my eyes, enjoying the lapping of the color on my hair.

Diane, in the meantime, is seated not far from me in the same stage of treatment.

I close my eyes and take a nap while the color is setting.

Forty-five minutes later, I am ready for my shampoo.

The stylist scrubs the color from my scalp. Shampoos, rinses, shampoos, rinses.

My eyes are closed.

Her intense finger massage feels delicious.

Done.

My head is wrapped in a turban to absorb the moisture.

Time to go back to her station for the blow-dry.

She removes the towel.

I put on my glasses.

I gasp in horror.

The stylist has dyed my hair Lucille Ball-red.

Auburn would be too kind a word for the color.

I think, *My lord! What am I going to do? I look like a freak!* I say nothing but do an internal primal scream.

As the stylist dries my hair, the color gets even more intensely red.

Diane catches my reaction and comes over to see me.

She chuckles.

"Oh, it really isn't that bad. I kind of like it."

Suddenly it occurs to me, in France, a popular color for hair is purple.

Why would red be unusual?

I slink out of the mall, catching glances of my new color in the reflection of the store windows.

As Diane drives me home, she tries to buffer me up.

I sneak glances in the side mirror of the car.

What am I going to do?

Next time I will be more specific, I decide.

Returning home, before entering the house, I call out to Patrick.

"Patrick, I am coming in now. Be very careful what you say to me."

He knows something dire has happened.

He looks at me.

His lips are pressed together; he's trying not to laugh.

He averts his eyes.

"Jackie, it will be fine. Remember, none of your friends in the States can see you now."

Small consolation for the *nouveau* redhead.

The next day I slink into school. My colleagues give me faint praise as they absorb the surprise new look.

The fire-red hair goes over great with the students.

Just one more weird thing this "*Américaine*" is capable of.

October

CHAPTER 30

Fashion Forward

THE WARM WEATHER STILL lingers into October.

Today the forecast calls for a sunny, cool morning, warming by mid-morning. I select black, open-toed sandals to wear with my black slacks and sweater.

Ready for school.

During my first hour class, my overriding thought is how cold my feet are since the morning chill does not dissipate, and as a further surprise, there is rain.

Patrick has driven me to work, so I have no option but to bear my fate and work during my free hours on lesson plans in the lounge rather than venture outside in my sandals.

My colleague, Sylvie, who has spread her work out on the grey rectangular table in the faculty room, looks up as I enter.

"Hi Jackie, how is it going?"

"I am still adjusting, but I think I'm making progress," I reply.

"Not to worry; it will come. At least our weather changing from warm to cool will keep the students more focused on school."

"So true, but I am afraid I have been surprised by the rain. I should never have worn sandals today!"

Sylvie stretches her spine, leaning over the edge of the table, to see my bare feet protected by thin strips of leather over a thin leather sole.

"Your feet must be so cold," she says.

"Oh, they are, but that's the way it goes."

"*Allons*, we have a good hour and a half. Let's go to the mall to get you some covered shoes!"

"I can't ask you to do that," I respond.

She slides her papers together, taps the sheets three times to even the edges, and inserts them into a folder which she slips into her black attaché case.

"My work can wait. Off to the mall we go!"

I weakly protest as I rise to stuff my papers into my locker.

"That is so kind of you, but it is really raining."

Sylvie smiles. "All the more reason to go!"

We dash through the courtyard to find shelter under the roof of the cafeteria.

My feet are sopped.

"You stay here; I will get the car and pull up."

Le centre commercial, the same mall where I got my color, is a short ten-minute ride from school.

Sylvie, who lives nearby, knows every entrance, so she parks closest to the retail area.

The rain has abated a bit when we arrive at the mall.

I follow Sylvie by jumping shallow puddles of muddy rainwater that have pooled in the uneven hollows of the parking lot, yet my feet still get wet. I leave my footprints on the tile floor of the mall as if I had exited the shower.

The shoe store is at the end of a neon-lit corridor.

The ladies' section is in the front. Colorful, slithery heels, loafers, and running shoes are displayed on large round tables.

The salesman who is emptying shoe boxes from large shipping cartons looks up and hesitates a moment to assure himself we are serious shoppers, worthy of interrupting his work, before approaching us.

After a brief greeting, I say, "I am looking for a comfortable pair of shoes in size 41."

He gives a Gallic guffaw before announcing that in France, that size for women is not easy to find, at least in his little boutique.

Sylvie interjects, "Surely you have something for my friend."

"*Désolé, Madame.* What you are asking is impossible for me."

"*Monsieur,* what do you have in my size in men's shoes?" I ask.

Sylvie gasps.

Without a reaction to this unusual request, he says, "Madame, follow me."

He leads me past displays of black industrial leather shoes with cotton cord laces, and business casual Italian crafted shoes with impossible pointed toes.

"I can offer you sports shoes. Here, for example, is a pair of black Vans tennis shoes." My cold feet prod me to try them on.

He disappears behind a curtain to his stash of shoe boxes and returns with a large black and grey cardboard box. The word "Vans'" is written in large font across the lid of the box.

I ask for socks and try on the black canvas shoes with the garish white laces.

The wide foot box and high rubber sole make my feet look like Bozo the Clown's.

"They are fine; I will buy them. Please wrap my sandals. I will wear these now."

With the purchase of mid-calf black cotton socks, Sylvie and I exit the mall.

My feet feel warm, secure, yet I sense I have disobeyed every foot-fashion rule of the French woman.

It is recess when we return to school.

Crossing the courtyard, I greet a few of my students.

At noon, as I walk through the lunch line selecting my salad, a colleague taps me on the shoulder.

"I hear you bought some new shoes."

"How did you learn that? Did Sylvie tell you?

"*Mais non.*" It is the talk of the playground that the *professeur américain* is wearing Vans.

Apparently, to my surprise, the brand name Vans, to the mind of a middle school student, is the height of fashion and snob appeal. However, I had never heard of them before.

To test the theory, I go into the schoolyard after lunch to chat with the students milling around before class.

Upon seeing me, a band of students approaches. They encircle me, three-deep, to see my shoes.

A student asks, "*Pardon.* Where did you get these wonderful shoes? They are *très* cool."

"I got them at the mall. Do you like them?"

"Oh, Madame, these are so in."

Another wonders, "Madame, when are you going to wear these shoes again?"

"On Fridays," I respond spontaneously, nodding to the American tradition of casual Fridays at work.

"*Oh, fantastique.* Next Friday. We will look for them."

"Hey, Madame is going to wear these Vans every Friday," a student cries out to relay the message to others.

This is big news to all the students in earshot.

In a small town outside of Bordeaux, in the courtyard of a middle school, I make fashion-forward news.

CHAPTER 31

And Then He Left Me

PATRICK IS SCHEDULED TO return to the United States on Sunday for three weeks. This will be the longest stretch of time he has been away from me.

I have been dreading his departure.

Although I have had a few good days at school, certain classes are still harrowing, and I often return home feeling beaten down.

I depend on Patrick to buffer me up, to listen, to advise, and above all, to be there.

His meetings are at a company in our town.

In addition to his work, he will have the opportunity to see Monique and Jean for dinner.

He does not want to go to our house, where they are now living, as it will seem strange and sad to experience being a stranger in his own home.

Fortunately, he has sisters nearby who will house their itinerant brother, so all is well.

All is well… except with his impending departure, I have great trepidation. This will be the first time I will be alone for an extended chunk of time, and every day at school poses unexpected challenges I am used to sharing with him at dinner.

I am also envious he can return to the States, see our friends, dine at our favorite haunts, and I must remain in France.

According to my agreement with the Exchange, I cannot return to the United States until the end of the school year. Maybe the organization is afraid an Exchange teacher might not want to return once home again.

"Let's play tourists this weekend and go to Cognac," he proposes, knowing a bit of distraction would do me good.

The city of Cognac is only an hour and a half northeast of our little town.

We choose local roads passing through endless miles of vineyards flanking either side of the rural highway. The rolling hills of *Le Bordelais* are magnificent on this fall day.

The leaves on the vines seem to be burning with crimson, gold, and orange-brown leaves, laden with plump purple grapes begging to be harvested. The air is balmy, the sun dazzling yellow against a cloudless sky. We think how blessed we are to be living the classic French life we have dreamed of.

At least, that is how I feel on Saturday.

We spy a small village nestled on a gently sloping hill. Its medieval stone church appears like a shepherdess guarding her sheep.

Its appearance has not changed for centuries, allowing us to imagine what a medieval peasant would have seen from his fields.

The entry to Cognac is marred by billboards touting its famous distilleries of liqueurs the French call *digestifs*.

We walk along the cobblestone streets of the old city of Cognac, stopping at the covered market, a corrugated building reeking of fish and red meat and poultry displayed in white steel refrigerated bins.

The songs of the vendors compete to entice us.

"*Allez*, come, Madame. Look at this chicken. It is waiting for you."

"Come see the freshest fish, still wet from the ocean."

We dodge shoppers wielding their carts through the crowded aisles to select fresh products from pyramids of peak-of-perfection fruits and vegetables.

There is an endless array of cheeses from which to choose. It is a wonderland of marvelous possibilities.

The markets whet our appetite for lunch.

We select a German-type restaurant, packed with locals.

Sitting in a hand-carved wooden booth, we dig into sauerkraut and spicy sausage as we watch the activity on the square.

A mother balances a baby in her arms and a child in her hand as she crosses the square; teenagers group on a corner, smoking and laughing among themselves dressed in their chicest black; two old men, seated on a nearby bench, reminisce. It looks like a movie set, all of them enjoying their Saturday, none sharing my dread of returning to class.

Returning back along the same route, we spy a castle from the middle ages. We drive up the approach road that circles the castle four times and arrive at the large double oak door.

A wooden sign at the entry of the château indicates the doors close at 3:00 p.m. We are a bit later than that.

The elderly guardian wearing an oversized grey quilted jacket and a navy beret is swinging a ring of comical iron antique keys as he starts to lock up.

With a *bonjour* and a smile, we tell him of our disappointment, saying we have always wanted to see the castle. We add that the visit will allow me to film the interior for my American students.

With a shrug of his shoulder, he directs us to park to the right of the impressive gate and follow him.

Clearing his throat, he rotely begins his patter about the history of this small fortified castle as I film every room.

The baronial fireplace in the great hall seems to still smell of pitch. Despite the warm day, the château is drafty, disabusing me of my fantasy of living in one like a princess.

We thank the guardian, buy a trinket in the gift store and tip him generously.

I am so pleased to have filmed the castle for Monique and our American students, many of whom have only seen a castle in a movie or at Disneyland.

We are on our way back home...to reality.

"Oh, Patrick. I am so going to miss you. It is really going to be sad being in the house without you. Do you have to stay for the extra meetings?"

I am only starting my poor-me litany of how miserable I am going to be without him, which I continue until we reach the house.

On Sunday morning, we set off for the airport. There is little traffic on the highway; we arrive early.

Patrick tries to cheer me up with small talk about what we will do when he returns.

He is looking forward to being back, seeing our friends, and being away.

I know it.

When we get to the departure area, I start in again with my woeful tirade. We notice his plane to Paris is delayed.

A stay of execution for me.

"Oh, great," I say. "I will go with you and have coffee."

My darling, patient husband looks at me and says, "Oh, that is all right. I have a newspaper to read."

He turns and walks away. I watch his red windbreaker until he is lost in the crowd.

CHAPTER 32

I Wish I Had Thought of That

THE DRIVE HOME FROM the airport is easy. No traffic whatso-
ever.

It is Sunday.

The French are home with their families, sharing a family meal,
followed by a Sunday walk or a lovely siesta.

I drive the car into the garage and close the doors. I am envel-
oped in grey-black darkness. The shadows of bicycles hanging from
hooks on the ceiling look ominous, the smell of gasoline from the
lawnmower noxious.

I am alone.

It feels good to be engulfed in the dark as if I am hiding my head
under layers of covers, snuggled warmly in bed.

I exit the car.

I open the door.

I walk into the kitchen.

Patrick's coffee cup is still on the table, half full.

I drink the dregs of the tepid brew as if to have communion with
one so absent, so far away.

What am I going to do? How am I going to manage?

My chest tightens as panic grasps me.

I have to get through this.

Taking a pad of paper and a pen from the counter, I sit down at the kitchen table to write a schedule of activities from the present moment until bedtime.

3:00 wash the lettuce

3:25 set the table

3:30 thaw the meat

The rhythm of writing the list calms me. As the day progresses, I check off each line item.

After dinner, I call Diane to check on the children; it reassures me I am not totally alone.

Every moment takes Patrick farther away from me.

We have always been other's shadow. Being with him completes my soul; I am totally whole when at his side. But now he is gone.

Just before bed, at 10:00 p.m., the phone rings.

It startles me.

Monsieur Girard excuses himself for calling me at home so late.

"Madame Donnelly, we have a situation we need to resolve by tomorrow."

"Madame Bisset has fallen ill and will not be returning until January at the earliest, and perhaps not until the second semester.

She has requested you take over her English class. You will teach her class until the end of the year.

Your current class will no longer study English but be assigned study hall.

Please stop by the office to pick up your new class list."

As he speaks, I think he has to be kidding. *Changing another class?* What is wrong with this school?

Madame Bisset apparently has a medical issue, which allows her to take a leave of absence for months. Having seen her a few days before, I have trouble believing she is ill, but I will give her the benefit of the doubt.

What a fantastic idea! She gets a paid leave of absence and

dumps me with her students.

I can't believe they are giving me another class of hellions in place of the ones I already had.

Why didn't I think of coming down with a vacation?

He finalizes his remarks, "I am sorry for the inconvenience, but I trust you understand."

"Of course, Monsieur Girard. Whatever you say. Thank you for calling."

I hang up the phone, stunned.

Typically, I would talk to Patrick about this. He would calm me, saying it would all work out.

He is flying over the Atlantic now.

I will deal with this alone.

The next morning, I pick up the new class list and immediately go to the discipline office.

The small, square office is the locus for the classroom aides called "monitors" who deal with student problems, oversee the courtyard, and supervise study hall.

The monitors are on break, slumped in chairs along the window, joking with one another.

Entering the room, they stiffen up as if a drill sergeant has barked, "Attention!"

"*Bonjour,*" I say warmly, to engage them collectively in answering the question I am about to ask.

I have learned that in France, you need to engage the person you are talking to with a little preamble of chit chat, or any request you abruptly make is taken to be rude.

I approach the closest monitor with my newly printed class list.

"Please highlight the students who will pose problems for me."

He picks up a yellow highlighter and runs his finger slowly down the page.

I anticipate the marker will delineate the names of half the class, as is the case with my other class lists.

"None, Madame. These students are highly motivated and should pose no problem for you."

I repeat my question lest my French betrayed me. He repeats his answer.

"None, Madame. I assure you this is an excellent class."

Leaving the discipline office, I feel a surge of joy that maybe, for three hours a week, I will be able to conduct class properly.

At 10:00, I wait in my classroom for the new students to file in.

They enter the class quietly and find a seat.

They unzip their backpacks, remove their books and notebooks and look at me expectantly.

"Oh, my, this can't be true," I say to myself.

I mentally thank Madame Bisset for taking her leave of absence and leaving me such a wonderful group of students.

"*Bonjour,* I am Madame Donnelly, your new teacher. I am American, here to teach you English."

Smiles sweep over their faces. They seem delighted.

"Shall we begin?"

CHAPTER 33

Another Day at St. Pierre

THE 10:00 CLASS I just inherited is the joy of my week.

It is for me a moment of peace. The students always have their homework done, are responsive in class, and appreciative of my efforts.

Their work is creative. They are a class that works well together.

For three hours a week, I feel affirmed that I can teach, that I am a good teacher. They are an island in a sea of trouble.

The other classes I teach, however, are composed mainly of students who have never been successful, so their group dynamic is challenging.

The most memorable is the class identified as "5/4."

"5" indicates the level of the class, in this case, 13-year-olds, and "4" is the section.

The class of 5/4 has an across-the-board reputation among teachers as being almost impossible to discipline because of a group of raucous boys who are not the least interested in learning.

In this particular class, there is just a handful of serious students.

However, one young man in this class, named Jean, is perfect. He has white teeth, bright blue eyes, hair styled just so, and a near-perfect average in English. He is stylishly dressed, not a smudge on his bookbag, quiet and obedient, a real learning machine.

He is so intelligent and capable; he can practically teach himself. He must have been placed in my 5/4 class through an error in scheduling.

Then there is René, a serious student who takes careful notes, tries to hear me over the chatter of the hooligans, and constantly raises his hand to volunteer. He is a victim since he and the other few serious students are underserved by my constant efforts at discipline instead of instruction.

Juliette is a mystery. She is a stocky girl with sad brown eyes and dark hair which she wears over her eyes as if to hide. Her seat is next to the wall. She leans her head against it, chewing her pencil and staring at me during class. What is she thinking?

When I approach her, she recoils. It seems there is something in her past that makes her frightened of adults.

There is so much about her I would like to know.

Vincent is the ringleader of the gang of boys. He swaggers in with his buddies, looking for ways to be disruptive. His friends follow his lead. Some are Romani, gypsies, who speak to each other in their own tongue.

I learn early on not to turn my back on the class for any length of time. Spitballs or crumpled paper could fly through the air.

My solution: I find a desk projector, onto which I write the lesson on transparencies while facing the students at all times.

In this cast of characters, there is one student who stands out as more memorable than all the others.

Alina!

She is barely five feet tall. She wears her long ponytail dangling down her back or knotted on the top of her head, depending on her mood.

She has a high, screechy voice that reaches even higher octaves when she gets excited.

Alina's self-appointed role is social director of the class; everyone is aware of her presence.

Entering the room, she passes from student to student, to check out what her friends are wearing, gossip a bit, or tease by lightly hitting over the head with a book.

Alina is a perpetual motion machine.

When I am at the board explaining a point of grammar, Alina will start her chatter.

"Alina, silence!"

"Madame, that is not fair. Paul is talking, and he does not get in trouble. Why is it always me?"

Yes, Alina, why is it always you?

What she does not know, and I do not share since I don't want to reinforce her behavior, is I find her unique and very likable. If she would only behave…

There are other students in this class whom I will never know well. They do not want to engage at all with me despite my efforts.

Yet I am intent on teaching them all.

I plow through the lesson above the interruptions and the chatter.

Most memorable is the day I am working with a student at his desk and hear a resounding thud.

Alina has fallen to the floor near her seat.

She is in a fetal position; her eyes flutter and close.

She does not move.

"Move back, students. Give Alina some air," I say as I rush to her.

"Delegate, go to the office! Report what has happened." The student representative elected to leave class on official business quickly leaves the classroom.

Alina is still.

The students are agitated and upset.

"Stand back. Give her room," I say forcefully.

"Madame, is she dead?" a student asks.

'No, of course not," I reply firmly, but I am not quite sure why she appears unconscious.

The doctor arrives. Fortunately, it is his day to be on campus.

He crouches down, examines Alina.

He takes her pulse.

He moves her arms.

He lifts her eyelids and looks into her eyes.

Standing up slowly, he turns to me.

"Madame, there is nothing wrong with her."

He extends his arm to help Alina up.

She rises slowly and sits back in her chair.

She smiles.

Alina chose to insert a little drama into the lesson.

Just another day at St. Pierre!

CHAPTER 34

Heroes Come in All Sizes —Enter Martin

Commuting home is beginning to get easier. I take to spinning around traffic circles, dodging the small cars weaving in and out of my lane.

Patrick is away, so I am not in a hurry to get home.

I love going through the town of St Vincent, noting which stores have sales, how many people are still selling at the market, then taking the last roundabout past our little shopping center, deciding if I should stop at Super U for salad and meat for dinner.

My home-free moment is the last part of the trip when the terrain turns decidedly rural. At the curve of the road, I am often stuck behind an oversized wagon, laden with hay draped over both sides of the truck, making passing impossible. I am not in a hurry. I am going home.

But this is not an ordinary day.

As I approach the gates, I am startled to see they are not closed as I left them this morning.

There is a tan Renault van in the driveway, its rear double doors are open.

A burglar! Do I drive by or accost him?

My curiosity is stronger than my caution. I pull up behind the van to investigate. A short man, with military-clipped hair, emerges from the open garage carrying a long garden hose. It is Martin.

Martin is Jean's friend, an associate at the store where they both work; Martin moonlights as a handyman. Jean has asked Martin to watch the house and be on call to do small repairs while he and Monique are away. If I was told this, I do not remember.

He approaches my car.

"*Bonjour!*" he begins in a rural southwest French accent.

"You must be Madame Donnelly."

"Hope you don't mind, but I need this extra hose for a job I am doing. A friend of mine is putting in a new vegetable garden, and his hose won't reach."

He slings the hose in the back of his van, wipes his hands on his jacket, and shakes my hand.

"How are you settling in?" he asks.

Without waiting for an answer, he adds, "I must say Monique and Jean's house is quirky and needs a bit of maintenance. How is the washing machine working? I told Jean to get a new one, but he is a stubborn guy. He keeps throwing money at it. Won't listen to me."

He smiles broadly, exposing his yellow teeth, stained from smoking. His faded red jacket is zipped open to reveal a white T-shirt beneath; his well-worn jeans are baggy. I notice he is wearing military-type brown lace boots; the thick rubber-grooved soles making his small stature appear a bit taller.

"*Bonjour*, Martin. So glad to meet you. We are enjoying the house, though it takes a bit of getting used to. Not quite like our house in the States, but it is fine, just fine."

I know Martin is not only a handyman but a family friend who is in direct contact with Jean and Monique.

He is there to offer help, but clearly, his keen blue eyes are casing the exterior of the house to report back to them how things look.

Knowing the house is spotless, I lure him into the kitchen so he can see how well we are maintaining it.

Inventing a pretext to prolong the visit, I say, "Can you tell me how to clean the filter in the dryer?"

He opens the dryer, removes the filter, taps out the small amount of lint, rinses the filter in the sink, and pops it back into place. He may have wondered why it is so clean after a few months living in the house if I didn't know how to change it, but he lets it pass.

I look at him adoringly as if he has just invented the wheel. He cannot help but send back a good report to Monique and Jean that we are taking care of the house.

Martin and I leave the kitchen and pass through the small patio to the garden. In rapid-fire French, he lists the flowers and the bushes, what they need in terms of water and pruning. "Don't worry, I will be back to trim them back before winter."

"Would you like a cup of coffee?" I offer.

"*Non, merci.* I have got to be going, but I'm glad to see you are happy here."

"Martin, can you please leave me your phone number just in case we have a problem?"

He reached into his worn wallet to give me his card.

Almost as an afterthought, he says, "Oh, I have something for you."

Sensing this is his exit line, I follow him out to the truck.

He rummages in the back of the van, pushing his derriere in the air as he paws through boxes, and produces a mason jar with a gooey orange substance.

"Here is honey I produce from the bees on my farm; I have 12 hives that I tend. These bees are very productive. I hope you like it."

I am so touched we have made a true connection through his visit and this gift.

Martin promises to return when I need him.

It doesn't take long.

Monique has jury-rigged a plug which barely covers the drain in the bathtub. Set on its side, it could slip through the opening. She attached the plug with a fine butcher's string to the faucet. She was quite firm in telling me, "Whatever you do, don't lose the plug."

It made me think of the monster movie: "Whatever you do, don't open that door."

It does not take me long to do just that. The string breaks, and the plug slithers down the opening in the tub.

Total panic.

Martin!

My hero arrives. He steps into the tub and kneels down.

With needle-nose pliers, he extracts the plug. As he works, I hover over him, wringing my clasped hands.

"I don't suppose you are going to tell Monique, are you?"

With a complicitous smile, he replies, "Why would I do a thing like that?"

With that, a friendship is born.

I solve future problems by buying the correct size plug at the hardware store.

I recognize, by the degree of my panic, I am actually quite afraid of Monique. There is no synapse between what Monique wants and what she expects others to do.

CHAPTER 35

La Suicidaire

EVERY MORNING WHEN I open my locker, I find notices of meetings, calendars of events, which change my routine and add challenges to my day.

In particular, just when I think all is moving along relatively well, I receive a polite summons to see the principal after my first-hour class.

What could this be? It is really too soon to be in trouble. Maybe some parents have been complaining?

At the end of class, I gather my record book, comb my hair, and set off for the administration building.

The secretaries, who have become like soothing mothers for me, greet me with smiles and warm *bonjours*.

"Madame will see you in a moment. How are you? How are the little ones treating you?"

After a bit of chitchat, the principal opens her door and beckons me in.

"Won't you please sit down?"

So much for the fast getaway.

"Madame Donnelly, we are very honored to have you with us. It is a rare opportunity to have a native speaker work with our English department, and I know the students appreciate your work."

"*Merci beaucoup, Madame,*" I reply.

If she only knew how much bedlam I deal with every day. My English teaching colleagues know English grammar better than I.

I really am a fraud.

Take a breath, Jackie.

"There is, however, a problem we need to deal with in one of your classes."

Okay, here it comes. Brace yourself.

"I don't know if you are aware there is a young lady in your intermediate English class who is suffering from a delicate mental disorder."

After what I have been hearing about the principal, I am wondering how she would know. Oh, boy, here we go again, I have a nutcase in my class. I don't know the kids well individually at this point, and they all seem a bit over the top to me....

"Oh, I will be happy to help," I say.

"She is a lovely young lady, quite bright, but her parents tell me she has fits of depression and might feel suicidal.

If you see any anxiety in her, please release her from class and have her come to my office. Her name is Céline."

"I will do everything I can to help. Thank you."

We chat for a few more minutes to embed the request into a social conversation, and then I leave.

Céline has never been a problem. She has brown shoulder-length hair, with straight-cut bangs; she's heavy into eye make-up, which gives her a bit of the Cleopatra look.

Céline sits in the back of the classroom; she is quite lively and chatty with her friends seated near her. There is nothing unusual or memorable about her behavior...that is, until she learns I am going to be of help to her.

The following class is, as usual, a struggle to teach, but the lesson is going well.

Suddenly, Céline stands up, puts the back of her hand to her forehead in a theatrical gesture, not unlike a 1920s vamp, and announces, "I am going to faint."

Usually, in my experience, people who faint don't stand up to announce they are about to lose consciousness, but Céline has a style all her own.

"Delegates," I call out.

The two boys, who coincidently are her best friends, pop out of their seats and walk her slowly to the door, each holding an elbow to support her as if she were eighty years old and doddering.

"Please take her to the office and be right back," I say, as I scribble out a pass.

Céline glances back at the class, looking amazingly well, and the three leave. The two delegates return 20 minutes later.

At the end of class, I inquire in the main office how Céline is feeling.

"Oh, she is fine. She sat with us and visited. Is there a problem?"

This theatrical scene plays out randomly for the balance of the year.

With the support of the principal, I have to let it happen. If there were an Oscar dedicated to a performance by an imposter, she would undoubtedly win it.

CHAPTER 36

Les Vendanges

JEANNETTE AND HER HUSBAND Vincent have invited us to harvest grapes at their small family farm where Vincent's father, Remy, moved upon his retirement.

The night before, Patrick and I lay out what we think will be appropriate *vendanges* clothes: old slacks, a collared shirt for warmth, worn tennis shoes, and windbreakers. I select a scarf for that jaunty French grape-picking look.

Vincent cautioned us everyone will begin to assemble at the farmhouse at 9:00 since we have a full day of work ahead of us, so we set out early.

The air is crisp, the fog reluctant to leave its claim on the low-lying fields of grapes. The earth smells musky; the soil, cold and damp with dew, seems to swallow the oxygen we are breathing.

I wait outside as Patrick guides the car out of the garage. I look up at the purple sky still dappled with stars and think *This is Bordeaux. I am in the heart of the wine country. What an honor to be here.*

Dark thoughts, heavy dread of Monday's return to work are far from my mind. I am living in the present; the harvest is my moment of reprieve.

With my sleeve, I wipe the dew from the windshield and climb into the cold car.

We take the highway, which passes through miles of vineyards. As we drive along the road, the fog lifts to reveal long rows of grapes plump for the picking.

We turn on to the smaller highway and see, off in the distance, St Émilion, the fairytale-like, medieval city we visited on that balmy day in August with Beth.

The church, with its tall stone spire, dominates the village. Cream-colored homes with speckled terra cotta and brown tile roofs cluster in random circles on the hills of the city. The rows of vines, symmetrically laid out, look like lines of corduroy.

This is wine country. We see billboards dotting each side of the two-lane highway, "Visit our vineyards. See how our wine is made. Producing fine wines since 1805." The stores are closed, the lights dim, the merchants who will later lure visitors to their boutiques are probably having breakfast in their small stone houses.

"Patrick, I think this is where we turn off. Vincent says we will see the narrow road beyond this small restaurant. There it is, turn here."

Patrick leans forward on the steering wheel to peer out over the dashboard. Being the navigator who never asks directions, he relies on his gut to find his way.

Slowing to a stop, he turns to me to ask, "Are you sure? This road looks like it is going nowhere."

I tap his shoulder and say cavalierly, "Let's try it; we still have time to get lost."

Taking a deep breath, which conveys, "I don't think so," he concedes and turns onto the dirt road.

In all our years of marriage, neither of us has chastised the other for getting lost. We think of it as a family trait, often leading to adventure and felicitous encounters with the unknown.

This time I am right.

The narrow road narrow curves gently around stone walls, delineating one property from the next.

A small wooden sign indicates the turnoff to the farmhouse. We drive past the village church, with a single rectangular tower, narrow slits for windows, and an imposing double door.

We are assured this is the right farm when we see Vincent's car parked in the small courtyard of the old stone farmhouse. Our arrival is announced by the crunch our tires make on the small stones of the driveway. After finding a niche to park, we alight and warily make our way to the farmhouse.

We pass a slanted, slightly warped, oak table flanked by wooden chairs, partially shaded by oak trees, in the courtyard close to the front door. *Oh, how dreadful it will be to eat outside*, I think, praying the sun will warm us before our midday meal.

Two cats are playing hide-and-seek, darting through the furniture before disappearing into the unkempt hedges. Chickens bobbing their heads in a staccato rhythm walk between us with arrogant indifference to our arrival.

Above the door, carved in stone, is the year "1703." We rap cautiously on the door, which is ajar, and enter the living room of the house.

Musty smelling books and magazines lean aslant on wooden shelves; a beige overstuffed easy chair, a round table, reading glasses resting on top of a leather-bound book, are in a nook of the austere living room.

Jeannette and Vincent, who are unloading a basket filled with food, greet us with pecks on both cheeks and present us to the portly housekeeper. Madame Cadert turns from the sink where she is peeling potatoes. She wipes her hands to dry on her apron before shaking ours. Her hands feel calloused and worn.

She has worked for Remy and his wife for 30 years. When Remy's wife died, Madame Cadert filled the void by taking charge of all aspects of running the property.

She supervises the gardens, barters at the market, makes minor repairs, and lovingly bullies Remy, who lives there alone, making sure he takes care of himself.

As we speak, our breath makes plumes of fog since the kitchen is chilly.

"O.K., *mes petits Américains*, are you ready to pick grapes and participate in the *vendanges?*" Vincent asks us enthusiastically.

Vincent tells us we are waiting for two other couples to arrive, friends from Bordeaux, professionals who like to play the peasants on the weekend by returning to the country. Vincent offers us coffee made in a speckled blue tin coffee pot, which is warming on the small stove.

"Jackie and Patrick, I want you to meet my father."

Vincent walks to the staircase and calls, "Papa, come down, please."

We hear the clumping of boots creaking on the dry wood above us. Step by careful step, Remy descends the steep, narrow staircase. Watching his shoes, then his legs, appear slowly, I wonder how old he is and if he is going to be pleasant to be with.

Remy stops at the bottom of the staircase to get his bearings. His gaze passes from Vincent to Jeannette. He smiles when he sees us.

He removes a woolen glove from his right hand to shake ours. Although in his late seventies, Remy is trim and farm-strong. A woolen cap hides his bald head; a scarf is wrapped twice around his short, stocky neck. He is wearing jeans, a plaid sweater, and a green oiled jacket worn for warmth since he lives in this house without central heat. A grey stubble of beard hides the deep lines created from years in the sun.

Apart from an occasional space heater, the giant fireplace in the living room provides warmth for his home. The scent of charred wood permeates the walls.

"It is a pleasure to meet you. We are touched you want to help us work today. I depend on my family and friends to do the harvest as I do not have any staff."

He continues, "We are a small vineyard. We deliver our harvest to the cooperative which processes the grapes into wine and bottles for sale. I am afraid you will be working all morning, so I trust you have had a good breakfast."

"Please help yourself to some whole wheat bread, butter and jam."

On the table in the kitchen are a rotund loaf of fresh bread, a serrated knife, a round plate of soft butter, and a mason jar of homemade blueberry jam that begs for tasting. Although we ate lightly before we left, we succumb to temptation, eating the buttered bread standing up, dropping crumbs which are caught by the hunting dog who lurks under the table.

Soon the two couples arrive. "*Bonjour!* Anybody home?" The friends walk through the door with accustomed familiarity, embracing Jeannette and Vincent, shaking Remy's hand and turning to us for an introduction.

"Welcome! You are a long way from your home in the States," quips one of them. "Are you ready for the challenge?"

Feeling not so sure of ourselves, but feigning bravura since we are personally representing America in this effort, and not wanting to appear like soft Americans, we assure them, "*Mais oui!*"

Gathering our gloves and hats, we set out for the vineyards, which are on a sloping hill behind the farmhouse.

There are two areas of vines divided by a pebble footpath. We will work the area on the right in the morning, and the remaining patch of vines in the afternoon.

Patrick and I are furnished *sécateurs,* grape cutters, rusty with wear. We will each work a line of vines which extends 25 yards along the slope of the hill. The others will do the same in their assigned area.

Vincent stands in front of us for our training. "It is really very easy. Hold the grape clusters in one hand to expose the spindly stem and snip! Then place the grapes in the basket."

What he does not explain is that to harvest the five rows of vines growing on wires supported by steel posts, we will need to kneel, bend, crouch, and stand to reach all of them.

As we fill our baskets to a reasonable level, we call for Vincent, who arrives bearing a cone-like container on his back attached by leather straps which loop under his armpits, and into which we carefully pour our harvest. He looks a tad like Santa Claus carrying his bag of toys.

Quick, witty banter bounces between all of us as we work.

The sun in its path becomes more intense, warming the earth. As it does, we enjoy the sweet, ripe fragrance of the fruit. Eventually, we take off our sweaters and jackets.

I am not very good at my job. The *sécateurs* are so sharp, and my skill so poor, I cut my index fingers and bleed onto the grapes. I muse that this harvest might take on a different taste, a full-bloodied wine.

The sugar from the grapes acts as glue to bind our fingers. And we work on.

This is not a make-believe harvest, a cultural activity for two Americans. No, we are working *les vendanges!*

Jeannette, who is stationed close to Patrick, speaks to him in English. She asks him questions about the States, what Americans think of France, how he likes St. Pierre, and what Patrick likes to cook. You really can't be in a conversation with a French person very long without the topic turning to food.

I, on the other hand, work near Remy, which allows me free use of my French. He explains to me the process of winemaking as we progress.

I know in large commercial wineries across France, the work of picking grapes is done by two-story-high massive machines that can strip grapes from the vines in little time.

But we are doing it the old-fashioned way, as was done for centuries past.

CHAPTER 37

Harvest Feast

THE SUN IS HIGH above us when the clang of the nearby church bells rings the Angelus. This bell tower has been calling the village to prayer at fixed times of the day for centuries.

I stretch up from my crouched position, straighten my s-shaped back, and massage my spine.

"*Allons enfants*, it is time to eat!" shouts Vincent.

This call is well met by all, who quickly abandon their grape clippers at their stations, as a reminder where they left off, and head down the narrow path to the farmhouse.

Madame Cadert has transformed the creaky rustic table into a regal feast by placing a faded red checked tablecloth over the uneven slats of wood. As appetizers, she set out trays of various *pâtés*, some of duck, others of goose; small cornichon pickles; mounds of freshly sliced soft French bread with crispy crusts; and smooth, wine-mustards which pique your palate and bring tears to your eyes. My favorite is the *moutarde à l'ancienne,* a mustard composed of ground and whole brown and yellow mustard seeds, mixed with sunflower oil, white vinegar, ground pepper, and salt.

Small squat glasses which used to contain grocery store jam, are set out on the table in front of bottles of red, white, and rose wines and Sauternes from the region. Some of the bottles have no labels, sealed by the waxy corks used by locals who produce the wine in their homes.

We use small oblong paper napkins as plates for our selections; but since we are standing, grazing around the table, our food meets our mouths quickly. Remy's dog is on high alert, poised to gobble up what is dropped, jostling our legs as he passes among us on his scavenger hunt.

As the wine warms our heads and our bellies, the conversation becomes louder and livelier. The group is bonding as a cohesive team of convivial friends united in a common purpose - eating!

Madame Cadert beckons us from the door to clear the table and bring the appetizer platters to the kitchen. She directs us to put the small dishes on the counter to the left of the sink. The platters are placed in a plastic tub in the large farm sink.

The kitchen, in the early morning, seemed cold and barren without the promise of a meal.

Now the smell of fine herbs, onions, and garlic emanating from the small oven quicken our appetites and our expectations of a French country-cooked meal.

Mme Cadert shoos us from her kitchen to the courtyard, after giving us each a plate and silverware.

We sit in anticipation, like obedient children waiting for a meal.

Our cook, who visibly appreciates her own cooking, waddles out, bearing a tray of cooked lamb garnished with potatoes and *primeurs*, the small, first-cut green beans.

She passes from diner to eager diner, serving us.

"*Non, non….* That is not enough, take more. You are too thin." Madame remarks to each of us, no matter what our body mass is.

"Who wants red wine? Oh, this is a really good white, try it!" are the refrains, as bottles of wine are passed from hand to hand around the table.

Are we really here? We will always treasure being part of the wine harvest of Bordeaux. My love of France, my love of the French becomes even more intense.

Patrick, who speaks limited French but understands everything, responds in English to what is bantered about at the table. The conversation flies from politics to fashion to family.

Madame Cadert returns, carrying a well-worn wooden bowl of soft lettuce glistening in an herbed vinaigrette.

More bread, more wine, more conversation in a centuries-old garden. We are part of an unbroken chain of life hidden among the trees encircling the courtyard. Are peasants from times past watching us, hovering about us, encircling us lovingly, welcoming us into this lineage?

I think how close we all feel to each other today, and how often artificial cultural and geographic barriers divide peoples. We all are human. We all want to savor life, enjoy our work and our families, and stay healthy. Is life really any more complicated than that?

If humanity could just sit down at the table together, might our differences melt away with the meal?

Soon Madame Cadert returns with a tray of cheese, some in square blocks, some in cut triangles, others round and soft.

"Ah, let me explain to you what these are," proposes Remy.

This is a Camembert; this a Brie; this cheese we brought from the Auvergne; that one is a Reblochon. Oh, you must try them all!"

I have learned from my French friends that how you slice the cheese indicates how refined you are. You never cut the point off a triangular slice of cheese but cut along the side. You may or may not eat the rind, depending on your tastes.

I slice along the side of an oozing Brie to the satisfaction of my new friends who might be thinking, *Ah, this American knows how to do it!*

A robust red wine is suggested as an accompaniment to this course.

Our postures change from being poised over our meal, to leaning back on our chairs, to give our bellies some more room, rather like how we feel after a hearty Thanksgiving meal.

Remy slowly stands, looks around the table at his guests, and says, "I want to thank you so much for sharing this day with me. The tradition of this vineyard dates back hundreds of years. Our small tract of land has, in part, produced the wine of Bordeaux, which is our very blood. Some years have been better than others. We fear drought, we fear too many rains, and we fear above all not timing our cutting so that, inadvertently, the frost comes and wipes out our entire crop."

"But this year, *mes amis,* I believe we are going to have a great crop, and I thank you for your hard work."

"I want to especially thank our Americans who have joined us today to be part of the *vendanges.* France and America have had a long history of helping each other in need. May I propose a toast to Patrick and Jackie! *Salut!*"

A short, clipped round of applause peppered by *Salut! Welcome! Bravo!* meets our ears and touches our hearts.

Madame Cadert leans her body against the doorframe, listening to our banter, her contented hands resting on her round hips. She turns and disappears into the darkness of her kitchen only to return with small round pots of *crème au chocolat.*

As full and contented as we feel, we have room for this superb finale: a touch of velvet chocolate.

"A *digestif* anyone?" Remy proposes a twenty-year-old cognac to top off the meal, which many, but not all, demure. "OK, then a *petit café?*"

At 2:00, we end our meal and head back to our work, our steps a bit slower than the fast pace of the morning.

Remy walks up the hill with me. "Let's work this tract together, shall we?" I retrieve my *sécateurs* and basket and join him at this new row of vines which is farther away from the others.

Remy retired from teaching a few years ago. He worked as a science teacher for thirty years in a local middle school whose students came from farm families.

Remy stops his work and turns to look at me, saying softly,

"I am wondering how you are doing at your school. Are you finding it difficult to adjust to our system?"

We are side by side, talking in a conspiring tone, almost like a priest and confessor.

I am taken aback by his question.

I look at his kind blue eyes, his weathered face.

I want to tell him how I dread each day; how, driving to school, my stomach knots tighter and tighter as I get closer. Dare I tell him of my pain? Will he tell Jeannette, or does she already know more than I have let on? Should I be cautious in sharing the truth with him?

After all, I am an American. I mustn't show weakness and reveal I am not up to the job.

I give in to my need to share.

"Please know I am happy to be teaching there. I do not regret my decision to be here. Yet I find it hard. I just don't feel in control. The students seem to be running the show. I never had this problem in the States."

Without pausing in his work, he sighs, "Ah, this is a problem. You are at a very difficult school. It has a reputation throughout the Bordeaux school system as being a troubled one."

He adds, "You must be clever. You must be one step ahead of your students. They must not be able to anticipate what you are going to do."

His advice is more troubling than consoling.

"Remy, I feel as if I am on a merry-go-round. No matter how hard I try to catch up, the gap between my students and me never seems to shorten. I can't seem to reach so many of them, and I fear they don't seem to want me to."

Remy pauses, thinking about what I have said.

"Then it is too late, my dear. There is no other solution."

He and I have exhausted the subject. We talk about France, vacations, and other pleasantries, but as we chat my stomach begins to tighten.

After a few more hours, the work is done.

We return to the farmhouse.

Madame Cadert proposes we stay for supper.

After such a spectacular meal, we wonder if we will ever be hungry again, so we decline the invitation.

We are tired. It is getting late.

Patrick and I take our leave, returning home delighted with our day of working the *vendanges* and our feast of delicious farm fare in the company of Jeannette, Vincent and their friends from Bordeaux.

However, this pleasant feeling always ebbs away.

CHAPTER 38

Screaming Mimi

SUNDAY NIGHT COMES AROUND, as it always does, and I am filled with gut-wrenching dread of the week to come.

This malaise usually sweeps over me in the early evening as I write my lesson plans.

How can I construct a lesson plan that will work? My 5/4 class has had a negative social dynamic in place since the onset of school, predestined to undo my efforts. My other classes are challenging, but not this impossible.

I know these behavior problems did not start with me. The rebellious students have been unsuccessful throughout their academic experience.

They have little expectation of success. School for them has been a series of failures. By now, they have already decided, "Why bother?" Also, their basic understanding of English is so sketchy, they have no foundation to build upon.

I have come to realize Monsieur Girard has clumped these kids together so as not to sully the other classes, and why not give these kids to the American since if she doesn't succeed, it really won't matter?

But I persist.

My lesson plan: First ten minutes, warm-up and review of the previous lesson. Next 25 minutes, transition into the meat of the lesson, last 10 minutes, small group activity. This should work.

But it doesn't.

I put the lesson plans in my briefcase, lay my purse and coat on my desk. I am ready for my departure in the morning.

At dinner one Sunday night, I push my food around the plate.

I am discouraged.

"Patrick, there has just got to be a way to regain control and really teach English."

"Jackie, look, it can't be that bad. You know what you are doing. Tomorrow will be fine."

"Honey, in a civilized world, you would be right. These kids are so uninvested in school, so pushed along from year to year, they don't believe they can succeed."

And then the idea comes to me.

If kindness and empathy do not work for these students, I will become a shrew.

Ah, I could hardly wait for the next day.

As the students in 5/4 burst into the room, I bellow, "Sit down."

Lest the message be lost, I scream, "Sit down NOW!"

The sound of my voice is heard through the walls.

The ring of boys who usually act out stop to look at each other, as if to say, "What is happening here?"

Walking toward them, I shout, "Sit down now and be quiet. Do you hear me?" Funny question, since I doubt no one on the second floor could not hear me.

They sit.

"Take out your work .... NOW."

The students comply. They are mute.

I bark the lesson. They obey.

They must be thinking to themselves, "Finally, we have a real teacher."

And so it goes in all of my rascal classes. Scream; threaten; obey. Repeat. Scream; threaten; obey. Repeat.

This strategy works brilliantly.

For the first time, since the start of school, I am in complete control.

Even Céline, the would-be suicide girl, who consistently threatens to faint in order to leave class, says, "You are giving me a headache."

"That is not all you will have if you do not get busy," I quip.

What a dream week. All I need to do is be nasty.

The students fall in line. I leave school every night happy with my day. I eat a good dinner and sleep like a dream. Life is so good.

This strategy is not applied to my wonderful 10:00 class, however. No need, since they are cooperative and productive.

But, alas, late Friday afternoon, I lose my voice and realize I cannot keep up this stress on my vocal cords until the end of the year.

I will have to go back to Plan A, since Plan B, *Scream*, will no longer work.

But for five fabulous days, I am a success as their English teacher.

November

CHAPTER 39

Doctor's Visit

PATRICK HAS AGAIN GONE to the States for meetings.

The weather turns grey and cold as the sunny fall days take their exit with an, "I won't be back, so don't ask where I went."

After Tuesday's classes, which I barely survive, I leave school.

I do not want to return to an empty house just yet.

To decompress, I decide to drive around to distract myself. Maybe I will go to Super U to kill some time, going up and down the aisles reading labels and buying stuff I don't need.

Or maybe I will drive through the vineyards, getting lost just for fun.

I feel like I am in a stupor, a combination of fatigue and confusion.

I drive through our town on autopilot.

I mechanically turn left off the main avenue and find myself heading to the doctor's office.

It is totally unplanned.

I have been here before to get a prescription for Patrick.

The office is in a grey stone house attached to a larger row of buildings. The doctor's office is distinguished only by his name engraved on a small bronze plaque hung near the right of the entrance.

I open the door.

The waiting room is stark. Two chairs flank the wall on the right; a low coffee table is devoid of the usual worn magazines one might expect. The late afternoon sun flows through the lace curtains covering two rectangular windows.

On the wall are three black and white photos of vineyards from the early 1900s.

Workers with jaunty hats and cigarettes dangling from their mouths are guiding grapes into big vats. At least they know what they are doing; and at the end of the day, they will return home to their portly wives, enjoy a good red wine and a hearty meal. They will sleep from the fatigue of the day, with not a thought of tomorrow.

That is not the case for me.

At every given moment, I am obsessed with this job, which I can't seem to handle.

Even a good glass of wine has only a fleeting amnesiac effect on me.

One other patient waits in the office.

The door opens. The doctor leads a woman out of the office and walks her to the door.

As he prepares to greet the seated patient, he sees me.

"Oh, how are you, Madame? Do you have an appointment I forgot about?"

I am a bit uneasy speaking in front of the other person. "No, Doctor. I thought I might stop by to see you if you have time."

"But of course. Please wait."

The doctor escorts the patient in. The door closes.

What am I going to tell him? I do not even know how I got here. I feel like I am on a conveyor belt being transported unconsciously toward a predetermined direction.

Patrick would be surprised to know I am here.

I rehearse my story while I wait. I want to explain my heavy heart, the raw fear, the blow to my ego that I am not strong enough to deal with this teaching job.

When I do sit down in front of this kindly country doctor, it all comes out.

"I can't do this anymore. The students are uncontrollable. This is October. I feel dry and empty. Oh lord, how I wish I never decided to do this."

"Where do you work?" he asks.

I tell him the name of the school. He sighs, "Ahhhh."

The doctor leans back and waits until I say every possible thing, emptying myself of my burden.

He thinks for a moment. Arranges some papers on his desk, then says, "There are not 36 solutions to your problem. You either stay or you leave. Or I will write an order giving you permission to leave your post for a month or more until you feel like you can return."

The French system allows for a *congé médical,* a work release written by a doctor.

He reaches for a pad of paper.

What a temptation.

It would be so easy. I could stay at home, watch television, and hide.

Oh, how enticing that would be.

No, I can't do that.

I am an American exchange who is here to do this job.

"Think about this, Madame. You cannot go on like this."

I clench my purse in my fingers, stand up, and thank him.

"What do I owe you, doctor?"

"Nothing, Madame. Your problem is not medical. I wish you luck."

I leave the office.

Driving home, I replay the conversation like the tune of a favorite song.

Breathe, Jackie.

As I enter the dark house. I turn on every light.

I blare music.

I receive solace from my little home.

Tomorrow I will go back to work.

Sometimes sympathy is medicine enough.

CHAPTER 40

Swimming in Deep Water

ONE OF THE ELEMENTS of French education, which is new to me, is the phenomenon called the *Conseil de Classe*.

Three times a year, teachers of students in a division like my 5/4, for example, meet formally to discuss each individual's overall standing, any adjustment problems, or other issues each student might be having.

In preparation for this meeting, the educators who teach these students English, art, history, math, science, and French, for example, have to fill out a pithy comment about the academic progress and behavior of each student in their class, in a two-inch space beside each student's name…in French.

This would merely be a clerical task for the French teacher. It is a fright for me as I have to compose a brief message in perfect French and in teacher-ese as well.

Fortunately, the International Exchange Program provides teachers with a page of possible remarks from which to choose.

"Pierre, although attentive in class, appears weak in his composition skills."

Since I teach five groups, each with approximately 25 students, this is a lot of work fraught with potential failure.

What if I make a mistake? Is my handwriting clear enough?

The forms are available the week before the meeting. During that time, there is a monastic silence in the lounge as each of us fills out the documents.

The grade sheets are also distributed for us to fill in.

Once the information is compiled, the schedule of divisional meetings is set.

I then return to school on a given night to meet in the all-purpose room with my colleagues to discuss each student in that particular group.

The challenge is to speak teacher-ese French. I want to sound professional. As my colleagues describe their students, I write down their turns of phrases so I will sound better when it is my turn.

Instead of saying, "Jean is a lazy student who just doesn't care," I now can say in French, "Jean does not demonstrate any desire to improve. There is a disappointing lack of application evidenced in his work."

Using this copycat system, I get up to speed quickly.

Before we begin the meeting, we are given an across-the-board printout of each student's grade for this group, so we can see how the student is doing in all subjects.

In France, 20 is the highest grade a student can receive. Some teachers joke that even God could not earn a 20.

The excellent students will score 18 or 19.

Defying mathematical logic, 10, which might be considered 50 percent of 20, and thus failing, is, in the French system, a passing grade.

My challenge is to make sure my students, the excellent, average, and poor students, fall within these parameters. My excellent 10:00 a.m. class averages around 18, the weaker students range from 7 to 10, with some falling below that mark.

In the States, many teachers tend to be quite generous with their grades, "easy markers" is how we describe them.

I think I best not grade higher than my colleagues or there will be repercussions.

I am relieved to see my grades for each student are in alignment with the others within half a percentage point.

Parent-teacher meetings are another minefield for me.

Here again, in individual conferences with parents, I want to communicate clearly about the progress and behavior of each student.

How easy it would have been in English where I could speak with nuance about their child. I do manage to communicate well with them; however, not quite as well as I would like.

The parents who come to the conferences are sincerely concerned about the student's progress. The parents of the problem ones rarely show up for conferences.

It is an honor to meet the parents on this level, and I do enjoy the process.

I am touched when the mother of one of my quiet students shares with me in a conference, "I am not worried about my son's progress. He just asked me to come to meet you because you are so kind."

Throughout this evaluation experience of the *Conseil de Classe,* as well as through the parent-teacher meetings, I have gained great respect for my French colleagues. Their level of concern for each student, whether high-achieving or weak, impresses me deeply.

Another challenge I face daily in dealing with young middle schoolers is understanding their slang.

Not only do they not enunciate, but they use, as do their counterparts in the States, a lot of expressions that come and go like the style of clothing they like to wear.

Joëlle is capable of speaking very beautiful French when she wants but usually speaks with a heavy dose of slang.

Without her I could never have survived in St. Pierre since a schoolbook command of French would never have been enough.

I have picked up so much from listening to her. In the beginning, I almost needed a lexicon to understand her.

Le flic is a policeman, money is *le fric*, water, *la flotte*.

A plus is short for *A plus tard*, meaning *see you later*.

It seems ironic that the French who love to talk, abbreviate so many words, perhaps, so they can speak more rapid-fire.

Appartement is *Appart'*. *D'ac* for *d'accord* meaning o.k., *le petit déjeuner*, breakfast, is *le petit déj*, adolescents: *les ados*, and so it goes.

Without knowing these words, I would be lost teaching at St. Pierre.

Still, even knowing slang doesn't always protect me.

Often a student enters my class late, for example, rattling off his excuse.

I ask him to repeat what he said, under the guise that I did not hear it, but in my head, I am wondering what on earth he just said.

Repeating often does not help.

I have to fake understanding, saying *"Et bien,"* a neutral remark which could mean anything. Meanwhile, the students might be telling me the school is on fire, and I would have no clue.

In one class, I was standing in front of the class. A rude student who could not see the board said, *"Dégagez!"*

That sounds pretty, I thought. I remember the term from ballet to describe a rapid leg movement. But from the shocked looks on the students' faces, I knew this *dégagez* was not good.

After class, I ask Jeannette about the word. She says it means, "Get out of the way."

Ballet terms only take you so far.

So, this school year, I have learned to speak "teacher-ese," formal parent-teacher French, and casual French with a heavy dose of slang.

Parlez-vous français? *Oui!* But on what level?

Thank you, Joëlle, for preparing me for St. Pierre!

CHAPTER 41

Now Thank Ye All Here Present

I HAVE ALWAYS TAKEN Thanksgiving for granted. It was just a restful, four-day weekend to be spent enjoying the family, eating too much of our favorite homecooked food, and relaxing.

Thanksgiving has been diluted by blue-light, early bird sales, football games, and the retail countdown to Christmas.

But, in its purest form, Thanksgiving can be an enriching pause, a time to reflect with family and friends on our many blessings.

I never realized how much this holiday meant to me until I had an out-of-country experience.

In France, Thanksgiving is just another day.

I remember as a child watching my father pluck straggly stubs of feathers from a fresh turkey with clippers, as my mother set the table and shooed us outside to play. My grandparents, aunts, and uncles with our cousins, arrived around 1:00. Family time, warm hugs, more mashed potatoes than a child should ever eat. This scene repeated over the years. Loved ones no longer present, new family members taking their place, but the focus always centered on our family and the love we felt for one another.

Patrick and I decide to share Thanksgiving with my colleagues and students. Since cooking a dinner for everyone is not feasible, our plan is to make the most American fare possible: peanut butter and jelly sandwiches for everyone in the school.

Patrick returns a few days before Thanksgiving from the States, carrying five large jars of peanut butter, an American favorite which, at the time, was not available in French grocery stores. The closest gooey thing the French eat is Nutella.

The night before Thanksgiving, we set up an assembly line of loaves of bread, jars of jam, and peanut butter on the table in the kitchen.

We slather a piece of bread with the peanut butter and jelly, plop another slice of bread on top, and cut the sandwiches in fourths. We put each quadrant into a plastic storage bag; 150 in total.

The next day before classes during morning coffee in the lounge, I distribute the bags to my colleagues. The gift receives mixed reviews.

"*Merci,* Jackie. I will save this for later," demurs Monsieur Girard.

Many teachers are delighted by my gesture. The daring sample the sandwich right away.

Coincidently, on that day, the local newspaper is scheduled to interview me about my experience as an American teaching in a French school.

Monsieur Girard takes me aside to caution me I must be very careful about what I say, and above all, to relate that all is well at St. Pierre.

I have been warned.

The reporter asks me simple questions: how I like the school and what I think of French education, to which I answer, as directed, all is just wonderful.

He takes a picture of Laurence and another colleague holding their little sandwiches.

The polite but strained look on Laurence's face is telling; it could easily be implied, by the cautious way she holds the sandwich in her two fingers, that she has no intention of trying this concoction.

The sandwiches go over better with the students, as they have never been offered food in class by a teacher.

Some students warily take their first bite, often being their last, whereas others scoop up the uneaten portions their friends do not want to eat.

This gesture of sharing sandwiches is my Thanksgiving celebration with my colleagues and students.

Alina, in my 5/4 class, assumes the role of hostess and food distributor. She bops from row to row, serving her classmates.

"Ah, come on Sébastien, you have to try this."

"Paul, you want more, here you go."

René, my serious, quiet student, eats the sandwich as if it were communion, representing another step closer to learning English.

The ruffians in the class make their ribald remarks but eat their share.

As the day passes, my mind drifts to our family at home.

Beth, who is staying with her grandparents, enjoys the holiday but misses us; this is the first time we have ever been apart for Thanksgiving.

I can see her relaxing in her grandparents' home, redolent of turkey roasting in the oven; I picture her grandfather making the gravy, admire the beautifully set table my mother-in-law is known for, and I miss our family all the more.

We speak to her on the phone to reconnect for a brief moment on Thanksgiving.

Mark calls us from Japan, where he is working, to wish us "Happy Thanksgiving." We linger on the phone, taking pleasure in the sound of his voice. He, too, feels as estranged from home and the holiday as we do. He plans to eat sushi for his feast.

We have invited Jeannette and Vincent to be our family surrogates for Thanksgiving dinner.

The memory of the *vendanges chez* Remy is still so vivid in our minds, such a truly French experience, that we want to share a taste of America, on a much more modest scale with Jeannette and Vincent.

While I am distributing sandwiches at school, Patrick is performing miracles in the single-oven kitchen. We find a large turkey at Super U.

Patrick uses the bags of Pepperidge Farm stuffing brought back with him from the States, to which he adds herbs, spices, celery, onion, and his own special magic. He peels the potatoes, snips the ends of the green beans, makes his amazing gravy, and prepares a main course dish for Jeannette, our vegetarian friend, in Monique's little kitchen. He uses the electric grill on the terrace to keep some of the food warm.

Jeannette, our stalwart Scottish Presbyterian, is comfortable saying grace before the meal. Vincent finds this a lovely tradition.

We all add a litany of people we are thankful for, our parents, children, and friends, before digging in.

On this day, we have made Thanksgiving an international event in a little corner of Bordeaux.

I don't think I will ever gloss over the importance of Thanksgiving again; this one being the most memorable, memorable for knowing how much I treasure time with our family, memorable for an opportunity to share our gratitude with colleagues and students who are now a part of my life.

December

CHAPTER 42

Almost a Reprieve

As the school year progresses, my communication with Monique becomes less frequent and less productive.

I don't know if it is from the fatigue of teaching classes, or her edgy personality, but in each communication, she becomes more brittle.

For example, I call her from the city of Sarlat in the Dordogne, where we are spending the weekend.

I want to let her know I am filming the city so she can share it with her American students.

"Really, Jackie, I think your students think you are just being a tourist, rather than caring about how they are faring."

Where did that come from? Was I not supposed to find ways to bring France alive to my American students?

Is she jealous I have so many more exciting places to visit in France than she has in our town?

I suspect she too must be as overwhelmed with her adjustment to the American school as I am to my school in France.

I begin to see there is a difference, however.

Ana, the young lady who grieved to see me leave, writes that Monique "just doesn't get how to teach us. She is very impatient with us. She keeps talking fast, and when we tell her we don't understand, she repeats what she said even faster."

Ana adds, "She insults the students who are slower than her expectations. She arranges the seating, so all the struggling students are seated on one side of the room and the successful students on the other. She turns her back to the first group and only teaches the smarter ones."

And, "Kids who used to love French hate the course and want to drop it. They are so unhappy."

This grieves me.

The few times we communicate by email, Monique does not mention this.

I do receive little jabs in her emails.

"I hope you appreciate your lighter schedule. I work so hard and only get my French salary. That does not seem fair to me."

Monique knew that would be the deal. She visited the school and read the Exchange Teacher contract. These terms should not a surprise.

Perhaps she enjoys being a martyr. Perhaps she is deeply angry at the difference in schedules. Maybe she is exhausted. I do not know.

At least, despite her apparent unhappiness, she is realizing her objectives, since Roger and Jennifer are in an excellent American school and are becoming fluent in English. So on some level, she must be pleased.

I wonder how she is getting along with my American colleagues.

When my French colleagues ask me about her, I do not perceive any affection on their part, more their curiosity.

I do not share the problems she is having in my school.

Despite our strained relations, Monique and I do continue to exchange videos, thanks to Patrick.

So, at least in this respect, our exchange is working.

Patrick invites Monique and Jean to dinner when in town. Jean is the only one who accepts the invitation. Monique is not available.

There is trouble afoot.

Susan, the principal, who initially supported this exchange, calls me in December to say there is a possibility Monique is going to be asked to return to France.

She is receiving so many negative reports from parents who are upset with Monique's attitude and teaching that Susan has had to intervene to calm them.

"Honestly, Jackie, if I had known this was going to happen, I would not have approved the exchange."

Susan meets with her staff and shares their concerns with the president of the Board of Education, who is already aware of the problem. This is becoming quite an issue, radiating beyond the French classroom.

Equal to my sorrow and concern for my students and their parents is the guilt I feel for creating this situation by my decision to go to France. If I had stayed at home, continued to teach, this would never have happened. How selfish I must be. But I really hoped it would work out in the end.

This is not the dream I had anticipated. I long to see my students again, apologize for their treatment, and somehow make it up to them.

Susan calls again to ask me how I would feel if I had to return to the States in January.

I see a potential safety line being thrown to me.

What an honorable discharge that would be!

I could go home, sleep in my own bed, and teach the students I have grown to love over my years with them.

For the next week, Susan and I communicate daily, weighing the pros and cons of sending Monique back.

It is finally decided, Monique will remain at the school but will be closely monitored to help improve her teaching and give her support.

I must admit I am disappointed: I would have loved to return home. But I know in the long run, this is the best solution. Monique will get help to do her job better, which can only benefit my American students as well as make her experience more positive and enjoyable.

I must say, to be fair, I am not at all as competent a teacher of English as I am of French, but in my heart, I know I have never given up on my students here in France.

That is a point of honor.

I am trying my best to teach all of the students despite their reluctance or their resistance.

I worry about Monique constantly, wondering why this exchange is not successful.

I do believe some people simply do not have the ability to get along with others and to be responsive to their needs. They should never be teachers.

CHAPTER 43

The Christmas Tree

THE HOLIDAY BANNERS OF lights are strung above the highway in our town, spelling out *Joyeuses Fêtes,* an all-inclusive expression covering both Christmas and New Year's Eve, the equivalent of *Happy Holidays.*

Our house looks pretty drab.

We want to liven up the house, make it Christmas-festive for the arrivals of Mark from Japan, and Beth from California.

We find the perfect purveyor of flashy decorations: *GiFi,* the French version of a Dollar Store.

Since we have not even bought a poinsettia, we set off for this small box store, which is known for inexpensive, bordering on cheap, seasonal items as well as household goods.

We sweep heaps of Christmas decorations into our shopping cart, hoping to fill the void of being away from our American home at Christmas.

It is our attempt at creating a Currier and Ives holiday.

"Do we have an outlet in the space under the stairs for the Christmas lights?" I ask Patrick.

Throwing five packages of lights in the cart, Patrick assures me we can fake anything with extension cords.

"Do you think this four-foot angel is a bit too much?"

"Oh, more is more, Jackie. Add it!"

We pile boxes of decorations into our shopping basket.

That should do it.

We select little boxes of chocolates as gifts for the school secretaries, kitchen, and cleaning staff since, in our minds, Christmas is a shared feast.

We store all our holiday purchases in the nook under the stairs for the moment.

I drive Patrick to the airport the following day. It will be a short 10-day absence. I am not sad as I realize the next time I see him, I will be on Christmas vacation, so I cancel my usual sorry-for-myself routine.

The days before the Christmas holidays become more frenetic as the students dream of vacation.

I ask students to make Christmas cards at home using a list of English expressions.

I am overjoyed by their creativity and the beauty of their artwork. They have cornered the market in glitter and ribbons with which they adorn their cards.

We make sure we deliver cards to Madame Laubert and Monsieur Girard. It can't hurt to showcase the students' talent.

On our last day of classes before Christmas, I am touched to receive presents from many of my students: Christmas candies, candles, even a wool scarf.

Finally, the last class bell rings.

I, too, am on vacation!

Nothing now to do but decorate the house for Christmas.

The night before the arrival of the kids, I select a fresh Christmas tree at the Super U grocery store, the parking lot transformed into a fir tree forest of Christmas trees.

I select a six-foot tree, a bit scraggly, but it smells so fresh.

The merchants, who know me well, deliver the tree a few hours later to the house and install it under the stairs.

The trunk of the tree is secured to two eight-inch strips of pinewood nailed in a cross position.

I ask if they are sure the base is sturdy enough to support the tree. "*Ne vous inquiétez pas, Madame,*" they assure me.

I have never trimmed a tree by myself, but I have helped out all my life, so there should be nothing to it.

I take all of the garish decorations out of their boxes: shiny red, green, gold and silver ornaments; two twisted red and green spiral garlands, as well as the beautiful ornaments the students have made for me; and arrange them on the dining room table in the order I will use them.

Putting on some Christmas music, humming along, I am ready to decorate.

Now for the lights. There are four strands of tiny white bulbs which I attach end to end to make the stringing easier. I put them on the floor in front of the tree so that as I begin to drape them, they will be easy to manage.

Hmmm, I think, *this is how Patrick would do this.*

Taking the stepladder from the kitchen, I mount the steps with the string of lights.

I carefully wind the lights, layer by layer, branch by branch, weaving them in and out of the pine needles.

Really, this isn't hard to do at all.

Going to fetch the ornaments, I hear the crash. The tree has fallen forward.

Oh, my lord, I am so in trouble.

Setting the tree upright again, holding it steady, I turn it slightly, thinking it will be more stable.

Crash.

I am a total failure. The kids are coming to a bleak house with a pathetic tree fallen in action.

So, alone, discouraged, and mostly desperate, I call Louise and Paul, the air traffic controller friends from the *Résidence St. Pierre,* who have taken a liking to us and with whom we have shared several meals.

Louise answers the phone.

"*Bonsoir*, Louise. So sorry to bother you, but I have a little problem. The Christmas tree keeps falling down. Yes, it has a base, but it is not enough to support it.

Where can I buy a metal base for the tree?"

"Jackie, we don't have bases for trees for sale around here. We don't use them.

Maybe in Bordeaux."

"My kids are coming tomorrow. I will think of something. Thank you."

There is a pause.

Louise says, "We are expecting guests for dinner. They will be here in an hour and a half, but we will be right over."

"Oh, you can't do that. You are busy. I will manage somehow."

"No, we will be right there," she insists.

In short order, Paul and Louise arrive, carrying a plastic bucket, a plastic bag of sand, satin material, and a red bow.

When they see the tree, they start to laugh. The fallen tree looks so pathetic.

"Stand aside, my dear," Paul says. "Nothing is impossible for the French!"

He and Louise begin to work. She lifts the tree; Paul twists the flimsy pinewood off the trunk and sets the tree in the bucket of sand. Crouching down below the lowest branches, agile Louise winds the fabric around the bucket and secures the end of the material with a broad red ribbon and bow.

It looks fantastic and very professionally done.

They help me string the lights.

"Poof, *voila,* my dear. Now you are all set. All you have to do is decorate."

We have to run."

As quickly as they arrived, they leave, but in that short space of time, they have set my world back in its orbit.

Pouring some wine, toasting my friends, I resume the decorating.

CHAPTER 44

I'll Be Home for Christmas... Maybe?

THE TREE IS DECORATED and stands in the hallway, begging to be admired. Since Patrick is away, I have had more time to bake cookies and prepare this perfect little French Christmas.

With multiple trips to Super U, I buy more wine, more sugar, more food, all the while humming, "It's Beginning to Look a Lot Like Christmas."

The Super U mall is buzzing with Christmas spirit. Every storefront is bedecked with twinkling lights, a Santa Claus waves from the roof of the restaurant, and shoppers are in an uncharacteristically good mood.

As the Mamma of the house, it is my job to make sure this is a purely magical time for us all. I have to make this Christmas work.

I pick Beth up at the airport. We have not been together since September.

On our drive back home, I catch up on her classes, her dates, and the doings of her friends. She sleeps in the next day, as she is exhausted from the travel, the jetlag, and too many college holiday celebrations. But she is home.

Mark arrives the following day from Japan, equally on one

engine after the long trip. His tall, lanky frame stretches out on the couch to nap, just as he always has done at home in the States.

Seeing the two children, now adults, together, allows me to pretend it will always be like this. I feel like a mother bird with large wings encircling them once again.

At midnight I receive a call from Patrick; he is at the airport in Chicago about to depart and is very ill. He has the flu and feels miserable. A wretched way to travel.

When I pick him up at the airport in Bordeaux the following day, he is pale and so weak he falls asleep as soon as he leans into the headrest in the car.

Helping him into the house, with a soothing kiss, I put him to bed.

Christmas music, candles, and the sparkling colored lights of the tree chase away the winter gloom for the children, but they are no avail for Patrick, who is sequestered in our room.

To add to the drama, Anne, my French friend of thirty years, and her grumpy husband, Gilles, are arriving from Paris to share Christmas with us.

Anne is a tender-hearted woman whom I met when she was an exchange teacher in Philadelphia, where I first taught. She taught French in a nearby high school. I heard through the academic grapevine that Anne, the French teacher, was very lonely.

I reached out to her, inviting her to my little studio apartment for lunch. Our friendship was born that day. Throughout that school year, we spent time on the weekends together until she had to return to Paris in June.

Subsequently, she taught English at the American School of Paris before her retirement.

We have seen each other every year through visits in Paris, or in the States.

After I married and had children, she became Aunt Anne, a

sentimental addition to our family.

Anne, who is much older than I, has vivid memories of the war. Her parents left their home in Paris when the Nazi occupation seemed imminent and sheltered Anne in their family home on the Atlantic. Her father participated in the resistance, was discovered and sent to a concentration camp where he died.

She did not marry her curmudgeon husband, Gilles, until later in life.

Gilles grew up in the same seaside town, spoiled by an overly indulgent mother before moving to Paris.

He and Anne had known each other as young people on the Atlantic coast, as well as in Paris, but had never formally dated.

After his mother died, Gilles called on Anne in Paris.

After a date or two, he asked, *"On se marie?"* *Shall we marry?*

She accepted, as she was in her late forties, and had given up hope of marrying anyone.

For her generation, who saw so many young men die in the war, being a married woman was very important.

They live in Paris, and despite his complicated nature, she loves him.

He is like an old bear. He is gruff, he growls, but somewhere, deep down, hidden beneath the bravura is a tender heart. I have seen it, but not often.

Gilles and Anne are not staying in our little house, but at a creepy, old hotel, the only one in the area.

I pick them up from the train station and drive them to their hotel. I am a bit embarrassed when I see it.

The exterior white stone and brick are benign enough.

We enter the hotel through the double doors.

We see no one.

"Bonjour," I call out.

No one.

We walk through an entrance hall so narrow, I can almost touch both walls with my hands. Dated black-framed photos of nameless celebrities who haplessly spent the night at the hotel are hung on the wall.

We ring the bell on the small desk on the right. From the double curtains in the rear emerges a man, rather impatient to be interrupted from watching his soccer game, who registers them. He gives them the key, tells them the hours of breakfast, and disappears again.

Their room is on the third floor.

We climb the creaky, curving wood staircase at the end of the hall. Gilles carries the front of their suitcase, and I guide it from behind. We work to execute the sharp turn in the stairs. We look like movers negotiating a piano through a tight spot.

Anne follows behind, saying nothing.

The room has seen better days. Red and gold flowers dot the damask curtains, a pot of artificial flowers is precariously set on the white radiator. The bed has a sallow yellow chintz bedspread and two tired pillows. There is only one reading lamp on the right side of the bed.

The bathroom is small, with a porcelain sink, a bathtub with a flex shower head hanging low near the faucet. If by some chance, Gilles is not already grumpy, he surely will be after a night or two here.

Anne is tiny. She can fit in any space. She says nothing about the room lest she rile Gilles.

I bid them goodnight, hoping all will be well.

The next day is Christmas Eve.

Patrick is still ill.

Since we live in a rural area of vineyards and farm fields, there is nothing to do. Even Super U closes at noon.

I drive Anne, Gilles, Beth, and Mark to St Émilion for the day while Patrick is sleeping.

This visit to St Émilion is a far cry from our outing in August when the weather was warm and sunny, and the tourists abundant.

The wind from the ramparts of the city blows cold. St Émilion looks like a deserted movie set, with only a few stores and restaurants open, as most merchants are home for the holiday.

We find a café where we eat *sandwich au jambon* and have tea to warm ourselves. We pretend to be having a good time.

We drive Anne and Gilles back to their hotel to rest.

We return home.

Before we left for the excursion, I had set the table with the best dishes Monique had left for us to use, placing red candles at both ends of the table, and adding a few pinecones for decoration.

It is time to prepare the Christmas Eve meal, which in our family is, traditionally, very special.

Mark peels potatoes, Beth makes the dressing, I season the turkey breast and put it in the oven. My ill husband, who is still MIA in our bedroom, is not on hand to make his gravy.

We all are trying hard to make this Christmas work.

CHAPTER 45

Christmas Celebration of Sorts

ANNE AND GILLES ARRIVE in the early evening by taxi.
We sit in the living room by the fire, sipping an aperitif.

Mark and Gilles both sip *Pernod,* the anise liqueur Mark discovered on a summer visit to their home on the Atlantic.

The two of them are complicitous; they have a special bond. I suspect Gilles feels Mark is the son he never had. Gilles has always been very indulgent to him as he was growing up.

We ladies select a crisp white wine.

We exchange gifts. Gilles has brought us a bottle of Veuve Clicquot champagne; Anne, two silver candlesticks, which we put into action immediately and ironically will be a tremendous resource to us a few days later.

We sit down to dinner: oven mashed potatoes, cooked carrots, a large turkey breast and stuffing, salad, and of course, slices of always-delicious French bread.

This American menu does not please Gilles. He chats politely, interacts with the children, but never lifts his fork to try the fare.

Gilles has stringent gourmet expectations that are not met that night. He has perfected frowning from his eyebrows to his chin, in one sweeping motion. During dinner, he acts like someone waiting for a train.

He does enjoy the Pomerol wine served with the meal.

Anne, who is long accustomed to his behavior, says nothing.

When I serve ice cream for dessert, Gilles bounds back to life and eats two portions.

Before Anne and Gilles return to their hotel, she embraces me.

"Thank you, dear, for a wonderful evening. It was lovely. I love being with you."

The dishes are piled in the sink, the glasses still on the table, the roasting pan on the counter. They all can wait.

We are now alone. The kids and I decide to open our presents, which are stacked under the tree. There is no Patrick.

My husband is still hibernating in our room.

But we have Christmas presents on our mind.

We are in the living room. Mark uncorks a bottle of champagne as we sit in front of the fire.

Just one thing is missing.

"Patrick," I call out, "Are you alive? We are going to open our presents now."

From deep inside his lair, we hear a weak, "I'll be out."

Rising from his sickbed, cured by his hours of rest, he joins us in the living room. A chilled glass of champagne revives him. We toast being together again.

We think of our home in the States.

Before we left for France, we showed Monique where all of the holiday decorations were stored. We can imagine the tree by the window near the lake, and Monique, Jean, and the children sitting around the fireplace enjoying their Christmas. For both families, it is a new international experience. We hope it is a good one for them.

Here, far from our family and friends, in a little stucco house on the edge of a vineyard in Bordeaux, we celebrate being together.

CHAPTER 46

Christmas Day

WE HAVE MADE RESERVATIONS for our Christmas day dinner in the small dining room of the creepy old hotel, which, surprisingly, offers an excellent menu.

The day is blindingly sunny but very cold. The kids and I take a walk through the neighborhood to work up an appetite for an early afternoon meal as well as pre-burn a few calories.

We notice multiple cars in the driveways of our neighbors, families reunited for the holidays. There is a sense on this Christmas day that all really is calm and bright.

We meet Anne and Gilles at the restaurant.

Viviane, an English teacher colleague is divorced and alone for the holidays, so we invite her to join us. She is reluctant to accept the invitation as she does not want to intrude on our family meal but clearly is pleased to be with us.

This is going to be our treat, but as Patrick still is not feeling up to snuff, Gilles assumes the role of host, sitting opposite me at the table.

He is in his element.

After examining the six-page wine list, he selects a Bordeaux red and white for the table. Mercifully, he does not believe the most expensive wine is the best since there are many vintage bottles with hefty prices on the *carte des vins.*

He and Anne begin with a half dozen glistening oysters served on a bed of crushed ice. Beth and Mark, being more conservative, elect a shrimp cocktail served with a spicy tomato and horseradish sauce.

I cannot resist the lush, velvety *foie gras,* accompanied by triangles of toast and a sweet fig confit. I elect a glass of very sweet Sauternes to accompany the dish.

We order the garlic and rosemary-rubbed roast lamb, which is the proposed Christmas dish. It is not a hard decision since the compelling fragrance of the herbs and garlic is wafting from the kitchen.

Gilles eats it all.

The chef makes a personal appearance wheeling in a sumptuous cart laden with *Camembert, Brie, Roquefort, Munster, Comté*, and *Saint-Nectaire* cheeses.

He delights in identifying each cheese with a sensuous description of its taste and origin.

We point to our choices, which he deftly cuts for us.

The chef suggests a hearty red Bordeaux to pair with the cheese.

After the cheese course, we take a pause in our culinary adventure.

More wine, more conversation: this Christmas is starting to work out just fine.

The dessert menu is extensive.

Is there any question that the classic *Bûche de Noël* will win our hearts? It is a sponge cake rolled into a cylinder, filled and frosted with mouthwatering chocolate buttercream.

The waiter also brings out a cookie tray of French almond macarons, butterfly-shaped cinnamon *palmiers*, almond paste *calisson* candies, and of course, *canelés*, the small round fluted pastry flavored with rum and vanilla: the dessert specialty of Bordeaux.

At the end of this truly celebratory meal, we take our leave, wishing Viviane, Anne, and Gilles a very Merry Christmas.

Returning home, we recount to Patrick, in sensuous detail, every aspect of the meal we shared.

As a family, Patrick joins us to spend the evening together on the soft leather couch. We tell family stories on each other. Patrick and I remind the kids of crazy things they did as children. In revenge, Beth and Mark reveal mischief they got away with, due to their cleverness and our ignorance. Their impersonations of us bring tears to our eyes.

So much laughter, so much love; what a blessing: this Christmas of sorts, became a Christmas for real.

CHAPTER 47

On Second Thought

"HEY, HONEY. LET'S SEND the kids out for pizza tonight and have a quiet dinner together. They've been cooped up with us for the holidays. I think we all need some downtime," I suggest to my husband who is now totally on the mend.

We broach the subject to Beth and Mark. They are in agreement; they are ready to get out of the house. Pizza Napoli, the only casual restaurant in the area, is a 15-minute ride away.

Following my own advice, I take a short walk through the neighborhood in the late December afternoon.

The platinum sky is etched with charcoal wisps of dark clouds, the wind lightly lifting my hair.

As I walk, I notice the leaves beginning to dislodge from their hiding spots and swirl around my feet. The temperature is dropping; the air becomes colder, the wind more strident.

Light rain slants into my face.

I turn around and walk quickly back. A storm is racing me home.

The honey-colored light from the windows of our house contrast with the grey cover of night. I feel like one lost in the woods who suddenly finds the miller's house in the clearing.

I close the door quickly as the cold wants to follow me into the warmth of the house.

Patrick is reading in the living room.

"I don't think the kids should go out tonight. I am not feeling good about the weather," I tell him.

"We don't have enough chicken for them," he parries.

"Patrick, we will make do; we can stretch the dinner. I don't want them to leave."

I have a premonition something terrible is going to happen.

Mark and Beth, awake from their lazy afternoon naps, are amenable to staying home.

I dash in the rain to the garden to cut basil from a terra cotta pot. Returning, the door slams behind me. "This storm is really stirring," I say.

From the kitchen window, I see the boughs of the trees swaying, their wood groaning.

I shred the leaves from the thin stalks of the basil, brave remnants of the summer growth. Putting the plump chicken in the roasting pan, I season the skin with sea salt, basil, and pepper. Slicing an apple and quartering a lemon, I mix the ingredients and stuff the cavity to capacity.

Around the chicken, I put quartered pieces of potato, and carrots and baptize it all with warm, bubbling butter.

After an hour, the chicken and fine herbs fill the house with the smell of home.

"What's for dinner?" asks Mark, opening the oven to inspect the source of the aroma.

The candlesticks Anne and Gilles gave us at Christmas flank the green, red, and white Christmas centerpiece on the poinsettia tablecloth, a tad stained from the holidays.

Dinner is ready.

The children's faces are golden from the light of the candles.

The wind whirs and roars and catches the shutters from the upstairs bedroom like sails pushing them against the house.

The wind, like the wolf in the fairy tale, seems to take rhythmic breaths to blow our house down.

Throughout the night, our stalwart stucco home resists the assault. We, oblivious, think this is just Bordeaux in the winter.

CHAPTER 48

The Morning After

THE HOUSE IS COLD in the morning. No power. No lights. No coffee.

I open the shutters.

The trees, which line the drive, have fallen crisscross across the street like a pile of pickup sticks.

"Patrick, come here, you won't believe this."

He joins me in the driveway. Around us is destruction: cracked limbs, jagged trunks of trees, power lines draped against defeated utility poles.

In one night, hundreds of trees are uprooted, revealing the underskirt of their trunks entwined like a woven fabric.

The hurricane is unexpected. France does not get hurricanes, but she did.

We go outside to confer with our neighbors. We feel like survivors of the London blitzkrieg, going through the rubble the morning after a bombing.

We join Diane and Alex and walk around to the back of the house, where more neighbors are gathered. The Martin family, blessed with a camping stove, can cook. Madame Martin is drinking a large cup of coffee, the steam wafting toward us. I crave it but am too proud to beg for some. I never knew until then how enticing a cup of java can be in the morning when you don't have one.

Monsieur Martin has heard on his car radio no one can take the road to town. The fire department is blockading the street because the power lines are hot. The fallen trees prevent passage as well.

The kids awaken.

We dress in layers since the interior of the dark house is colder than outside, by about 20 degrees.

"What if we take the road in the other direction? We have to get to the mall to buy candles before nightfall."

We wedge ourselves in the car and set out. The road in front of the house is impassable. We find side roads. Just like following a maze, we turn right, turn left, turn around where tree trunks block a country road, driving miles in search of civilization.

Mercifully, we find the main highway leading to the large commercial shopping center.

We are relieved to see the parking lot filled with cars.

The mall has power. The supermarket buzzes with life as if nothing has happened. Shoppers blasély pass through the aisles, unaware of the horror we have seen.

"Stock up on anything we can cook on the grill. No need to worry about refrigeration."

In the hardware aisle, we grab flashlights, candles, and matches.

Like looters, we fill the cart.

Before leaving the mall, we decide to have our last hot meal in the Chinese restaurant, envious the mall has light and heat.

We return to our frigid home.

"How long is this going to last?" we wonder.

At first, it is an adventure, eating sandwiches in wool hats and leather gloves, reminiscing, enjoying being together again in the darkness, the crimson-orange flames from the fireplace warming our faces.

The laughter holds us together in the darkness and the winter cold.

We guide ourselves with candles to our rooms, rummaging in drawers to find more layers of clothing to wear.

"I found more blankets, who needs some?" Beth cries out.

At bedtime, like the Walton's, we call out to each other, "Goodnight, keep warm, I love you." "I love you too," echoes back in the darkness.

We choose not to keep the shutters closed, hoping the silver steel moon will warm the house.

Since the kids have another week with us, we want to make sure their holiday is not a nightmare of frozen faces and no light past 4:00 p.m.

Our firewood supply is almost depleted.

Fortunately, the city of Bordeaux is spared. We make reservations for two rooms at a modest hotel downtown.

We take three days' worth of clothing and some books. As an afterthought, I put the television-VCR that I use for my classes in the car, in case we want to watch DVDs.

We stop at the mall to buy the full series of *Friends*.

Driving to Bordeaux, we blast the heat to thaw our cold fingers. The warmth is delicious.

We settle into our lodgings at the hotel, thankful to have shelter since our St. Pierre house is uninhabitable.

The city seems to be in a state of suspension. There is a sort of let-down after Christmas. The sales at the stores have peaked, the after-Christmas promotions have not started. There is a lull before the festivities of New Year's Eve.

The grey of the day melds with the grey of the buildings. The cold wind barrels down the narrow streets. The lights of the restaurants and cafés cannot chase the gloom of the winter days.

We decide to hang out together in one of our rooms at our little hotel; the kids and I nestle on one bed, binge-watching Phoebe,

Ross, and Rachel and Chandler fall in and out of love with each other or with others while Patrick reads in the easy chair.

We only venture out in the cold to find nearby restaurants and then return to the welcome warmth of our hotel haven.

Patrick and I know tomorrow we must return to check on the house and to retrieve more clothes for our stay.

The kids elect to stay in Bordeaux.

Boy, this holiday is really a lot of fun.

CHAPTER 49

As If It Couldn't Get Worse

BESIDES NEEDING MORE CLOTHES, we have no Internet available to us to read emails at the hotel, so we must return to the house.

It is a Catch 22 situation: we need to charge the computers at the hotel because there is no electricity at the house, and return to the house to use the Internet, because there is no Internet at the hotel.

En route to the house, we blast the heat, hoping our bodies, like a thermos, will hold some warmth.

It is bitter cold.

Even during the day, despite the pale winter light streaming through the windows, the house is nearly pitch black.

In the semidarkness, the shadows of holiday decorations and the sagging tree seem to mock us, ghosts of Christmas past, seemingly an eon ago.

While Patrick reads and responds to email, I decide to take down the decorations from the tree to create some normalcy.

I put the snarl of lights and ornaments on the table more by feel than by sight. The only light in the house is the glow of Patrick's computer screen. When I am out of range of his monitor, I stumble into furniture.

The tree, except for the few ornaments I must have missed, feels bare.

What to do with this faithful witness to our lovely Christmas?

I have no idea how the French dispose of their trees, but I have the ingenious idea to burn it.

Dragging it out to the side area near the service door, I set it alongside the driveway on the pristine little white stones.

Using the skills afforded me by my scout days, I crumble old newspapers, paper towels, and a few stubs of candles to make the pyre.

I light the tree.

The smell of the pitch is delightful; the fire crackles, but the smoke blinds and burns my eyes when the wind changes.

Patrick appears at the door.

"Jackie, let's go. It is getting dark," he says as he prepares to lock up the house.

"Go get your purse and let's get out of here."

"Please wait. I have to finish burning the tree."

"We can do it tomorrow. It is almost burned out anyway. It is not going anywhere. We will leave the shutters open, so perhaps, with the sun tomorrow, the pipes won't freeze."

I really don't want to leave. It is a smoking charred mess, but I comply since I am bitterly cold.

We leave the tree half-burned in the enclosure, the ash from the embers soiling the white stones.

Apparently, moments after we leave, with comic timing, Monique's elderly parents arrive. Monique dispatched them on this spy mission to assess the damage from the storm and the condition of the house.

Apparently, they see the remains of the charred tree in the entry area, and the shutters left open, and enter the house to inspect the damage.

If indeed they could make out anything in the semi-darkness, it would be the heap of Christmas decorations placed willy-nilly on the dining room table.

The half-burnt tree, the shutters, and the disorder in the house get them very worked up.

Just as they feared, the Americans are not taking care of the house.

Confirming all their suspicions and fanned by the sight of such negligence, they will phone Monique in the United States to tattle on us.

I imagine Monique's father trying to calm his wife.

I also imagine Monique's mother feeling entirely vindicated that this teacher exchange was a terrible idea, and her daughter should never have left France.

While driving back to the hotel, we have no idea we are about to be in a lot of trouble.

January

CHAPTER 50

Now Hear This!

IT IS NIGHTFALL BY the time we return to Bordeaux. Like a camper, I still smell of smoke. It feels so good to be back in civilization…heat and light.

The kids tell us they went out exploring but now are happy to rest before dinner.

I think of Monique.

I am sure she has heard of the hurricane. News of the storm has been in the U.S. press since it is an unexpected phenomenon of nature. No meteorologist had seen it coming.

I decide to call her to let her know we are okay.

I want to put the best face on our plight. It has not been easy commuting back and forth to St. Pierre.

Living in a hotel has its drawbacks. The kids are adaptable and good sports about it, but our Christmas vacation is proving to be less than ideal.

I call from a pay phone in the lobby of the hotel.

"*Bonjour,* Monique. This is Jackie. I am calling to tell you we are all well. It has been quite the experience. Rest assured, we check on your house daily."

I wait. No response.

Suddenly, I hear her scream at me.

"What the hell are you doing? My parents just visited the house. It is a disaster.

The shutters are open, the Christmas tree is burning near the driveway. The inside of the house is a mess."

Silence. She is reloading.

She continues, "I am taking good care of your place. The least you can do is the same for me."

Louder still, "I can't believe you chose to leave. You should be living at the house. I don't care how cold it is."

"Monique, think about it. We have no light, no heat. We can't cook. We are doing the best we can under the circumstances."

I continue before she can comment further.

"Yes, Monique, I agree it is my fault about the tree. I didn't know how to remove it. I am sorry. It was a mistake. It will be disposed of soon."

"Sorry? I don't care if you're sorry." Her voice continues to rise as her rage at me increases.

"How would you like it if I treated your house like you treat mine?"

I don't think she appreciates our situation. She is calling from a warm house with central heating.

The man phoning in the open booth next to me can hear her screaming and turns around to stare.

Realizing I am nailed, and there is no defense since burning the tree is clearly my fault, I close the conversation.

"Monique, I will give you time to calm down. As soon as we get back to your house, we will take care of the tree."

"Goodbye."

Shaken, I hang up the phone. It has been a long while since someone has screamed at me.

It is too bad this has happened. It is even worse we got caught by her parents.

I can just imagine the graphic report her worrywart mother gave Monique.

It is indeed the perfect storm: the cold house, my bad judgment, the burning tree, and God help us, the open shutters, and the timing of her parents' spy mission.

I hope Monique will calm down and understand more about our situation.

Going up to our room, I hug Patrick and the kids.

Sighing, resigned I can do nothing more tonight, I say, "Let's go out to dinner."

CHAPTER 51

Best Laid Plans

Y2K, THE TURN OF the century, is anticipated with both great excitement and apprehension. Those who are optimistic, plan for celebrations. The cautious wonder if time, as we know it, will stop, if the computers will not adapt to the new millennial and disaster will follow.

We are definitely in the first group, anxious to celebrate this momentous event.

Our family plans to join Joëlle and her family in Meymac, a small rural city in the heart of France, for the big celebration.

Meymac is a classic, undiscovered French village with a town square, small shops, and a large stone church.

We spend months working out the details of the party we are going to co-host, which will include Joëlle's sister, daughter, neighbors, and friends who have become like family to us through our many visits.

We will drive three hours to join them on December 30th, which will give us time to get settled before New Year's Eve and finish the party preparations.

The town square with its prominent clock will be the Times Square, where the villagers will meet for the countdown of the minutes to the new century.

All is in place.

Except the hurricane has changed all of that.

The roads are closed between Bordeaux and Meymac, totally impassable due to the fallen trees.

Joëlle's town does not have electricity; there is no chance we can stay with them.

We are regretfully disinvited.

What to do?

Days before the event, we try to make reservations in local restaurants.

We are rebuffed. "Sorry, we have no room. You should have reserved earlier."

We are resigned to eating Hamburger Quick in our hotel room.

By chance, we approach a restaurant on a narrow street, which leads to the Garonne river.

We explain our plight.

"We can make room for you, Madame," the restaurant manager tells us.

"You must arrive by 8:00 p.m. to be done with dinner before the fireworks begin."

We are delighted.

At 8:00 p.m., in our winter finery of warm boots, down jackets, gloves and woolen hats, we arrive at the restaurant.

The *maître d'* has put us at a prime table near the window, from which we can watch the early bird revelers stroll in the street.

The napkins are set in a silver ribbon on a crisp white tablecloth; the wine glasses sparkle in the candlelight.

We are each presented with a rose and a glass of bubbly, and the evening's *prix fixe* selections.

To accompany the champagne, an *amuse-bouche* of snails in a dainty puff pastry is served.

As a first course, the choice is either a brochette of golden scallops sautéed in butter and garlic or *foie gras* and chutney.

The main course offers more options.

I elect the *gigot d'agneau*, a marvelous leg of lamb in a mint sauce; our son, Mark, the lobster and seafood medley; Beth and Patrick, true carnivores, the *tournedos Rossini*.

Each dish is garnished with scalloped potatoes, baked golden, creamy, with an oven-crisped top layer, and green peas with chanterelle mushrooms.

Ah, dessert!

Patrick opts for the *soufflé au Grand Marnier*; Beth and I, the fresh fruit crumble served warm, crowned with small mounds of whipped cream; and our son, a goblet of *mousse au chocolat*.

With coffee, the restaurant offers us a platter of chocolate *macarons*, nougat truffles, and chocolate mints.

The meal is seasoned with spirited recollections of Christmas holidays past. The kids teasingly remind me I can't get through a Christmas carol without crying and reminisce about the enormous 14-foot fir trees which, with the help of neighbors, we would place beneath our vaulted ceiling at home tethering the massive tree with wires.

We remember the grandparents, aunts, and uncles who spent snowy Christmas Eves with us, and Beth and Mark recall how the gifts they received as children were so special.

With French precision, we end this marvelous meal at 11:45 p.m., profusely thanking our *maître d'*, who made this family dinner forever memorable.

The warmth of the restaurant dissipates quickly in the cold winter night.

We join the crowds assembled for the fireworks at the *Place de la Bourse*, a complex of three buildings designed by Ange-Jacques Gabriel in 1739, on a large square facing the Garonne river. The symmetrical illuminated columns, so representative of classic

French architecture, loom over the square where we stand.

Before us is the future, the new millennium. Behind us, represented by the buildings, three centuries of history. Even more than our sense of celebration, we share a feeling of awe to be living through this extraordinary moment in time.

To be reunited in France for this historic occasion makes it all so much more magical.

I cannot help, despite the specialness of what we are sharing right now, counting on my fingers how many more days I have with the children, praying the time will go slowly; then, counting how many more months I have at St. Pierre before finishing the year, hoping those months will go quickly.

In so many ways, this evening is a parenthesis in time, a suspension of responsibilities and cares. The reality is these holidays won't last forever; we won't always be together.

The fireworks begin. They are set off across the river, orchestrated to be dazzling and dramatic.

The crowds chant *oh* and *ah* in unison. People of so many backgrounds, so many cultures, assembled in one wave of unity, celebrating together the turn of the century.

The finale or "*bouquet*" is overwhelming. The fireworks regale us with glittering red, white, and blue pyrotechnics, reminding us this is a French celebration. We feel the noise of the fireworks in our very bones.

Applause, shouts of *Bravo!* reverberate against the passive white stone colonnades which have seen this all before, and we hope, will continue to witness the passing of time, long after we are gone.

CHAPTER 52

That's What *Friends* Are For

THE HOLIDAYS ARE OVER. Mark and Beth leave on the same flight to Paris to reconnect with their lives far away.

Beth has packed French chocolates in her carry-on to sustain her on the trip back to California. Our son will fly through Paris to Japan. Fortunately, we are consoled he will be back at Easter. We will not see Beth until her graduation in June.

Our time with them has come to an end.

We will miss them terribly; their absence is wrenching. But they must leave.

Patrick and I move our things to a drab boarding house on the outskirts of Bordeaux since our home is still uninhabitable, as is most of the area. Electricity should be restored in a week or so.

The weather in January is a malevolent cold. The absence of the sun, the low grey clouds, chill us and add to our malaise.

The landlord lives on the first floor of this stone and stucco house. He has a quasi-nice dog who snaps at us if we do not drop toast for him at breakfast.

Our room is large enough for our suitcases and the portable television-VCR, which I will again take back to school.

Most of the area outside of the city is like a war zone.

Some areas have light, others are dark. The storm's path was random.

We learn many people have lost everything.

Patrick and I visit a large storage building commandeered to collect clothing, household goods, and food staples. The hands of the volunteers working in the unheated building are so cold, they fumble to receive our contributions.

The school of St. Pierre has power, so classes will be held as usual.

But it will not be usual to have students return to school in clothes borrowed from the shelter where they are staying.

Nor will it be usual to see the fatigue and confusion in the eyes of the returning students. Many are living through the trauma of devastating loss: their homes and all their possessions taken in the flooded Garonne.

I will be told, with gallows humor, "Madame, I don't have my books. They floated away down the river."

On the first day back to school, Patrick carries the television up to my classroom.

Re-entry after a long vacation is always daunting, but with the stress of the hurricane, it is even more challenging.

I plan to show a video of a pep rally Monique filmed at a time when we were still communicating.

My third-year English students take their seats. They are not unruly: they are exhausted.

After taking roll, I press "play" on the machine. I think the exchange video will keep them occupied for 15 minutes while I get settled.

There is a gasp, then a shout of joy.

Unbeknownst to me, I have left an episode of *Friends* in the VCR.

I hear cries of delight from the students. "Phoebe!" "Ross!" "Chandler!" "Rachel!"

These television characters are indeed their friends.

They know their personalities, their antics, and their history.

The students' eyes are alert and lit with joy.

I never got that reaction from the English lessons in the textbook when I would ask if Miss Pritchett ever found the keys she lost.

I look at them.

They are so engaged. It is one of the moments teachers live for: when a real connection happens between the students and teacher in a shared learning experience, even if by accident.

Building on their enthusiasm, I ask questions about each character.

Where do these friends live?

What instrument does Phoebe play?

What kind of job does Joey do?

The English flies out of their mouths because they are talking about people they care about.

They eagerly explain they are fascinated to see American life and love the Central Perk Café.

I know what I have to do.

That evening I start binge-watching every episode of *Friends* to find those not sexually explicit. This will take me weeks to complete since, in every episode, there is usually some sexual situation or innuendo.

I fast forward through the four-box series, and eventually, find 16 episodes suitable for class.

I write the English curriculum so that each episode, shown in small segments, will become their English lessons.

As they listen with interest to the conversation among the characters, they develop listening comprehension.

Answering questions orally about what the characters talked about develops their speaking skills.

Writing the answers to my questions improves their writing skills.

Using the series, I can work in the grammar they need, and keep them happily engaged at the same time.

Although rewriting the English curriculum represents a lot of work for me, the pleasure of watching the kids learn is so worth it.

The students at this level are now excited about their English class.

The drama of Miss Pritchett's lost keys is put aside for the living life stories of our "*Friends*".

CHAPTER 53

A Change of Command

THE LAST TIME I saw Madame Laubert was before Christmas vacation. She made rare appearances around campus; she knows she is mostly ignored by the faculty who are preoccupied with last-minute responsibilities before Christmas. We have *Conseils de Classe*, missives to parents, and overall crowd control of students, who are more than primed for vacation.

I had bought a small gift for Madame Laubert at *Gifi* when we bought the Christmas decorations. It is a rectangular notepad and pen wrapped in red paper with a gold ribbon.

I want to give it to her personally, so I slip into the administration building between classes.

The secretaries greet me warmly.

"What are your plans for the holidays? Are you going back to the States for Christmas?'

Sadly no. We will be here.

"May I see Madame Laubert? Is she free?" I ask.

"Of course."

Her secretary, wearing a dress of seasonal red and green, rises to accompany me to the door of her office.

I knock, then enter.

It, of course, makes sense to knock on her door as it is closed.

I find it strange, however, that at St. Pierre, one knocks on every door, even the library door, which is always closed.

"*Bonjour,* Madame. I don't want to disturb you, but I wanted to see you before vacation begins. I have a little gift for you."

She rises from her desk and walks quickly over to where I am standing.

Her face looks stricken. She is not accustomed to receiving a present or being singled out in any way.

Extracting the present from my purse, I offer it to her.

She opens it carefully, preserving the paper to be used another time.

"Oh, this is so kind of you, Madame," she says warmly.

I shall put this on my desk and think of you."

"You are welcome. I hope you have a lovely holiday and I will see you in the new year."

As she thanks me again, her voice trails.

I detect there might be a problem but dismiss it as my imagination.

The first week back at school, the faculty is in survival mode. The teachers' lounge is abuzz with stories of where we were when the storm hit, who has electricity, who doesn't, and how we will help our students through their reentry to school.

Many, like us, have been displaced by the hurricane and are in temporary housing.

Monsieur Girard, who usually does not spend time with us minions, sits in the lounge listening to our stories.

He is uncharacteristically in an up mood, finding any opportunity to join the conversation.

This is strange; we soon find out why.

Bruno, who has valuable contacts in the central office in Bordeaux, announces, after Monsieur Girard has left, that Madame Laubert has been relieved of her duties and is no longer principal.

Monsieur Girard is in charge until a replacement is found.

Perhaps his euphoria is due to the hope he will take over as principal.

In any event, for a week or so, we are rudderless. It makes no difference since Madame Laubert has always been absent physically and certainly was never at the helm as an active administrator.

On the third Monday of January, an announcement is made that we have a new administrator who will be introduced to us at a meeting at noon that same day.

We dread the worst. Who could this be? Could it be Girard? That would be no one's choice.

Assembling in the community room, we wait.

Monsieur Girard appears at the door.

He escorts a woman who is very attractive and beautifully dressed. She has an expensive haircut, stylish light pink wool suit, and matching heels. She is no Madame Laubert.

She passes by him, walking briskly to the front of the room.

"*Bonjour.* I am Madame Colbert."

"I have been assigned to St. Pierre because the central office believes this school is at risk. The leadership has been problematic; the strike unacceptable.

I look forward to putting the school back on its feet with your participation.

I respect the leadership and skill of the faculty. That has never been in question."

We are silent.

We take her in.

We now have someone in a high position from the central administration in Bordeaux, who is competent and forceful.

Delight!

"If there are no questions, we will get back to our duties. I look forward to meeting each of you personally to find out how I can help you do your job. We are all working together for the common good."

Monsieur Girard, who was not invited to stand beside her as she speaks, stays in the back of the room.

He has met his match.

February

CHAPTER 54

Here, Take a Seat

ONE OF THE PREMISES of good teaching, featured in most methodology textbooks, is that firm and consistent discipline creates a solid basis for learning. This statement seems pretty obvious. Methodology books are full of self-evident advice written by college professors who have probably never set foot in a middle school classroom.

The factor that makes this information even more unusable is the theoretician has never met my students.

For example, in my eighth-grade class there are two oversized young men who have obviously failed a year or two and are older than the rest.

They have been together through the years and are obviously a bonded pair.

André is blond, bright-eyed, and shorter than his buddy Luc, who is six feet tall. André is very malleable. He follows Luc through all of his adventures, but I sense he would never have the wit to act out in class on his own. He is a great sidekick and audience for Luc.

Luc, on the other hand, is the most trying student to handle in this class.

He has a show-me swagger, sitting with his long legs extended in front of him so he can trip someone passing by, has a penchant for burping loudly to accentuate a point I am making, and makes other mysterious bodily noises. André and Luc are inseparable, kind of a Frick and Frack act.

I realize that to create a positive atmosphere for learning, these young men need to be separated.

On page 132 of *How to Teach Effectively*, it states that before disciplining a student, one should talk to the student privately, offering options to solve a given problem.

All discipline, the book goes on to say, is more effective if done discreetly.

So, in this case, following this advice, I will take Luc aside to suggest he voluntarily move away from André.

Confident this strategy will be effective, I approach Luc before class. He is slumped against the wall in the hallway, waiting for the bell to ring.

Looking up at him, I start by telling him how glad I am he is in my class, and I hope he is enjoying learning English. I then slip in, "Oh, by the way, I would like you to move away from André and find another seat in class where you can concentrate more on your lesson. You can select any empty seat that suits you."

He curls his lip in a snarl, which I take for agreement.

The students file into the classroom, unaware of the *entente* that has just been reached.

Luc lags behind. He strolls slowly into the classroom. André follows. They take their seats together.

"Luc," I say, in my most mellifluous voice, "please find another place to sit in the classroom today."

Silence.

Luc stands up. *Victory*, I think.

Luc begins to growl. His eyes travel around the room. He finds an empty seat, picks up the chair, and starts to lunge at me. He reminds me of a lion tamer; he only lacks a whip to crack at me.

"You cannot make me do that!" he screams. Worse, and untranslatable in English, Luc has used the *tu* form with me, which is used for family, friends, children, pets, and in my case, someone you find inferior.

A student should never use the *tu* form with an adult in authority. It is tantamount to calling that person by his first name.

At this point, the students are watching gape-mouthed, stunned by what is going on.

I feel the heat of my blood rushing up to my face. This situation is not covered in the how-to book I cited previously.

Fortunately, my classroom communicates with my colleague Jeannette's by a shared door in the back of the room.

I walk there decisively, open the door, and ask Jeannette to come into my classroom. Because of the volume of his voice, she and her students are undoubtedly well aware of our confrontation.

"Pardon me, Madame," I say to Jeannette in a very controlled, angry-afraid voice, "please advise me. Do students threaten to throw chairs at teachers in France, and do they use the *tu* form with an adult?"

Jeannette responds this is indeed not at all normal and that she would take Luc into her class until he can control himself.

The door closes.

His buddy, André, who is the straight man for Luc's antics, has his nose in his book. He dares not look at me.

We continue the lesson.

The following day, I have a meeting with Luc and the new principal, Madame Colbert.

Luc and I are seated in front of the principal, who asks Luc to describe the situation. I have never seen anyone flare his nostrils so effectively as Luc does.

He does admit that perhaps he was out of line but insists I was unreasonable, asking him to change seats since he did nothing wrong.

The principal leans back in her chair. She stares at him quietly. Luc squirms. He wiggles his fingers on the arms of his chair.

After a pause, Madame Colbert tells Luc to apologize. He flares his nostrils again before reluctantly, and insincerely, apologizing.

Luc is dismissed.

The principal turns to me and says, "Please don't take him seriously. He is pure drama. I am sorry this happened."

I digest her words.

I clearly do not understand this young man. I did indeed take him entirely seriously.

"Madame, please just know one thing. If anyone hits me, I will leave this school."

Madame Colbert listens.

She accepts my conditions.

However, she assures me this will not happen again.

I leave the office. My knotted stomach slowly releases the tension I feel.

I believe I need to write an addendum to the methodology book I cited.

Evidently, the author has missed something.

March

CHAPTER 55

The Betrayal

BY NOW, I AM used to the clever little tricks my students use to cheat in class.

They turn to one another to borrow *Blanco*. Then a glance is all it takes to scan the friend's test paper.

Too alert to fall for this ruse, I devise an ingenious plot to thwart my little bandits. I create two sets of tests that look amazingly similar but for a small dot on the corner of version A which distinguishes it from version B.

The first question on each test is the same.

Then, in class, I hand out alternate versions, so they do not know the tests are different.

It works very well, unfortunately too well, as it leads to one of my most painful memories.

Pierre and Jacques, two nice kids, were absent one day from class. They are compliant, attentive students, and do not act out in class. They are very easy to teach.

When they return to school, they need to take a make-up test. I send them into Jeannette's classroom to do so, as this is our mutual system. They sit next to each other in her class while she teaches and take their test.

I give each one a different version.

Unfortunately, the temptation for dishonesty is too strong, and while Jeannette is teaching, they use that opportunity to cheat off each other.

Aha! I catch them. I proudly mention my technique to Monsieur Girard to show him how clever I am. Instead of unabashed admiration, his face tightens. He tells me we have to have a meeting with these brigands.

"Oh no, that is not necessary. I can handle this myself, thank you."

He insists.

The meeting is scheduled for late in the afternoon the following day.

Pierre and Jacques enter his office, heads down. They sit to my right.

Monsieur Girard stares at the boys as if they have committed murder.

I did not want this to work out this way. They are really good kids, quiet, polite, but caught in my web.

I am hoping the outcome of the meeting is simply to give them a warning that cheating is not honorable, and they should reform their ways.

I would have been satisfied with that.

Instead, Monsieur Girard says gravely, "I understand from Madame Donnelly that you have been rude and abusive to her."

My heart pounds.

Time stops.

I never said that.

The two boys look at me in disbelief.

At that moment, any trust we have established through the year disappears.

They believe I betrayed them.

I am heartsick.

I feel my face flush.

I am betrayed by this man who is absolutely indifferent to my relationship with these students.

My mind races.

What can I say that will not contradict my administrator but will still put balm on this situation, which is clearly out of control? What in the world is Girard thinking? Why did he put me in this position?

I breathe into my remark: "You are fine boys; I enjoy having you in class. I have only a question for you: Can you say you have always treated me with the utmost respect?"

The question is meant to affirm what the administrator is saying and yet not devastate the young men.

They squirm in their seats. Pierre says, "It is true we could have been kinder to you."

Jacques nods his head in agreement.

Pause.

I add, "If you promise to make an effort to be more cooperative, I am willing to forgive this mistake in judgment. Promise me you will do your own work from now on."

Monsieur Girard seems satisfied.

I do not think he has the sensitivity or the compassion to understand what he has done.

I am furious with him.

I shake the students' hands and smile at them.

"You really are good kids," I say.

But I think: *You have been sold out by a man who could not care less about you. But I do.*

I will somehow make this up to you.

CHAPTER 56

Training Obélix

MY RELATIONSHIP WITH MONIQUE has definitely taken a turn for the worse. In any email she feels compelled to write, she now signs her name, *Madame Aubin*.

It is almost comical. The era of the telegram is revived, as Monique measures each word in her missive to relay what she needs to say in the tersest style:

Where are the conversation books stored?

Madame Aubin

The ideal exchange we both hoped we could do has fallen apart, and now we lead parallel lives. I am as adrift in her world as she is in mine.

My colleagues at St. Pierre continue to ask about her. I have to make up responses.

"Oh, she is doing just fine," I say, as if I knew anything about her.

Reading the emails from my American students and American colleagues, I am getting more and more upset.

My impression is Monique seems to be shutting down, getting her job done, but perfunctorily. Any guidance Susan offers does not seem to be having a lasting effect.

I am sorry this is happening to Monique but moreover, I am concerned about the well-being of my students.

I am the only French teacher at our high school, so I have had many of these students for three or four years. I know them all well and feel protective of them, almost as if they were my own children.

I appreciate how hard it is to teach abroad. I know it is stressful for Monique to step into a different mindset about teaching, but I wonder if she couldn't be kinder?

And as much as I am suffering at this school, I will not give up on the students under my charge here.

This worry and concern for my American students intensifies as the year goes on.

In the neighborhood, there is a hefty, dirty dog called Obélix.

He is named for a character in an immensely successful comic book series called *The Adventures of Astérix*.

Astérix is a Druid who lives in the only village the Romans cannot conquer in all of Gaul, now France. He is spry and resourceful.

His buddy, Obélix, is a good-natured, but not too bright, giant, known for his brawn, who likes to transport huge boulders for Astérix.

Together they go on many adventures to the delight of the French children and adults who adore this series.

Our neighborhood dog, Obélix, is aptly named. He is massive and seems not too smart.

We love dogs, so we enjoy seeing him skittering through our yard.

Obélix is not very socialized but he is a sweet dog. When we try to pet him, he shies away.

He is the only animal in our life in France, so we welcome his presence.

We know Monique does not like dogs of any kind, to put it mildly.

We cannot help ourselves. We devise a plan.

Every night at dinner, Obélix habitually crosses our garden, perhaps hoping for some of the food he can smell emanating from our kitchen.

One night when he passes, we throw some meat to him. He eats it.

The next night he draws closer. He is rewarded with a piece of meat.

We repeat this every night until he has lost his fear of us.

Soon, we lure him into the kitchen with more raw meat.

"Come, Obélix. Come here. Good boy."

Obélix enters the house warily, his muddy furry paws marking his path on the white kitchen tile, his matted brown fur smelling of musty leaves and musk. Obélix drools long strings of saliva, anticipating the meat. He gobbles up his reward, mashing it with his large yellow teeth.

We repeat this practice every night at dinner.

From then on, every evening, Obélix circles our yard like a shark sizing up its prey.

"Come, Obélix."

Now, we put a piece of meat in the garbage can.

He retrieves it by knocking over the can, spilling the contents onto the floor. He steps on the tin cans, vegetable clippings, and broken eggshells spewing out of the bin, spreading them about.

The next evening, we put another piece of meat in the can. Obélix retrieves it.

In a short time, Obélix is trained to enter the kitchen and topple the can to get his treat.

Although it is a chore to clean up after Obélix, we find it so funny.

I relish the thought he will continue to visit when Monique is back in the kitchen.

She will know why this is happening.

Obélix will be the payback I need for the woman who seems, according to all reports, to be mistreating some of my students.

April

CHAPTER 57

The Funeral

THE END OF THE day always seems like a triumph. The students, quick to respond to the bell, cram their books into their backpacks, then tensely wait like bulls at the gate to be released.

The weather is unseasonably warm. The spring sun is still new to its job of warming the earth.

The students are impatient to be outside; slinging jackets over their shoulders, they leave the building anxious to savor the rest of the day.

"*Au revoir et à vendredi,*" I say above the fray. "Don't forget to do the assignment. I will be checking."

A few students, usually the same three girls who love to hover at my desk, linger to chat.

"I speak English at home, Madame," one shares with me.

"Can you tell me what this Beatles song means?" another asks.

"I am going to Paris next week. I am so excited."

I listen to their banter as I collect study sheets, grade books, stray pieces of chalk, a black eraser which has left a layer of snow-white dust on my desk.

Their chatter reminds me of my seventh-grade days when I loved to be near my teacher.

Sister Angeles was a tall, young nun. A crisply starched white cotton guimpe framed her beautiful face. She smelled of soap and warm wool; her black habit, perfectly pleated, made her look more like a storybook doll I played with rather than a real person.

I loved her unadorned hands, which extended beyond her draping black sleeves. In my eyes, she was perfect. I wanted to grow up to be as beautiful as she was.

Am I that role model to these girls?

As we chat, the girls suddenly become quiet.

Monsieur Girard appears at the door.

He stays in the door frame until he is recognized.

"Ladies, I would like to speak with Madame Donnelly right now. Have a nice afternoon."

The girls take their cue, gather their book bags, and leave.

Uh-oh, what have I done? What could he possibly want?

"Madame, a sad situation has developed. Your student Georges has lost his father. We are not clear as to how he died. I don't know if you are aware Georges lives with his mother. The family situation, shall we say, is most complicated. Georges will not be in class for several days. A few students have asked to attend the funeral. I will provide you a list of their names shortly."

"I would like to attend the funeral as well if I could be excused from my classes," I say.

Monsieur Girard replies, "That is not necessary, but it might be a good idea to have some faculty representation."

The assistant principal taps my desk with his knuckles as if to punctuate a thought, turns to leave, and stops.

He looks back at me, hesitates, and says, "That is really very nice of you."

Georges is a boy whom I hardly know. He sits in the back of the class. Stocky, short for his age, simply dressed, he has a buzz cut. In class, his brown eyes gaze at me with a *Please leave me alone* look.

Georges does very poorly in English. He seems to take his bad grades as a confirmation of the low image he has of himself.

Georges reminds me of a painted figure in the back of a large tableau, his face in the shadows, just a suggestion of a human being.

The next day, when Georges' class settles in, the students seem to be no different. His seat is empty.

"As you know, Georges' father has died. I plan to attend the funeral. If any of you would like to drive with me, let me know after class."

The class stirs uncomfortably. Students look at each other to see if anyone volunteers. No one.

After class, the students file out, bumping each other to get to the door.

Alina lags behind.

Alina says, "I would like to go to the funeral. My two other friends would too. Can we go with you?"

"I will clear it with the vice-principal and let you know later today."

Permission is granted.

The next day, Patrick drives to school with me to pick up the three students.

Alina organizes the seating. "I will sit in the middle. Emilie, you sit near the window. Edith climb in last."

As we pull out of the school parking lot, the students are silent.

I turn around to the three in the back. I am curious how they are handling what might be their first funeral.

"Did you know Georges' father?" I ask to break the ice as we are all quiet.

"I saw him once pick Georges up from school," Alina volunteers.

As we drive to the next town, we pass a gypsy settlement. There are vans, small trucks, campers, arranged haphazardly in a field. Laundry hangs from antennas and on lines strung from trees to cars.

Some of my students live here.

We arrive at a small, grey Romanesque church. We park in front of a flower shop. In the window are displays of floral funeral arrangements and gravestone markers, for a one-stop-shop from funeral to cemetery.

The day is spring-like but not as warm as before. The clouds swirl together, separate, and rejoin, producing a somewhat sunny day.

I am surprised to see there are so few people at the church.

The first few pews are occupied by family members.

They talk among themselves. George is seated with them; he stares straight ahead.

The European casket is perched on sawhorses a few feet from the altar steps. It is pinewood, crudely made, and inexpensive. There is a bronze crucifix screwed onto the head of the casket.

On either side of the bier, stand two modest wreaths, one bearing the message, "To our friend" and the other, "You are not forgotten."

Dusty light shimmers through faded stained-glass windows. Small votive candles flicker in tidy rows on an iron stand. The statue of the Virgin Mary on the left, Saint Joseph on the right, stare down impassively at the congregation.

On the walls surrounding us are rectangular stones embedded in the wall with the names of wealthy parishioners who were benefactors.

There is a massive bronze plaque with fifty or more names of fallen young soldiers, "*Morts pour la Patrie.*"

The organ groans a *dahdedahdah* music, which resonates through the stone walls.

The priest enters.

His vestments are silver and black. He is flanked by glassy-eyed altar servers in white no-iron surplices. The priest welcomes us as brothers and sisters, extends his condolences to the family, and rushes through the service.

We process out.

Where is Georges? Is he with his mother? We find him alone in a corner of the church's large portal. The family, milling on the stairs in the front, seem to have forgotten about him.

Georges is as invisible to them as he was to me.

My three students walk up to him and give him kisses on each cheek. He kicks some dust with his foot, his head bowed. He turns away from them.

Alina persists. The students communicate short expressions of sympathy and then are silent.

Patrick and I approach.

"*Bonjour,* Georges. We are here to be with you today. We are so sorry."

Georges looks up to see me. A smile passes his lips, then retreats. He never thought a teacher would come this far for him.

The wooden casket borne by neighbors is placed in the hearse.

Georges' mother retrieves him, greets us briefly, and leaves with the others for the cemetery.

We also leave to find our car.

The students obediently sit in the car in their assigned places. The talk now is intimate.

We talk about Georges.

We talk about loss.

We talk about things so tender as only this bonded moment could allow.

The solemnity of the service, the casket, the tears, are new experiences for the three.

We are sure they are absorbing what a devastating experience it would be to lose their parents.

Alina asks a lot of questions in the car.

What does it mean to die? How to do they prepare the body? How deep do they bury the casket?

We remember how we felt as children as we started to learn about death; it is such a frightening part of life.

Alina and her two friends are visibly affected by the experience.

We drop the students off at school after the funeral. They thank us for accompanying them to the ceremony.

Alina puts her head through the window in the car where I am seated.

She says quietly, "*Merci, Madame.*"

She turns and leaves.

But something has changed.

Alina and her friends will relate to me differently for the rest of the year.

We have shared an experience that has united us.

CHAPTER 58

Alina takes Command

THE FOLLOWING DAY, ALINA pops in to see me at lunchtime. I am working in my classroom.

"*Bonjour, Madame.* I have been thinking of you. You are a good teacher, but kids are taking advantage of you. It's what we do."

She takes her bookbag off her shoulders and puts it on the floor near my desk.

"Madame, you need to change some seats if you want peace."

She asks for the seating chart, leans on my desk, one leg crossed around the other ankle, and begins to work.

"The whole problem, Madame, is that groups of friends are sitting way too close to one another. You don't know who they are, but I do."

She begins to draw arrows where this student should not be close to that one.

"Don't tell anyone I did this for you," she asks.

She picks up her backpack and leaves.

The next day, the students are somewhat lined up outside the classroom door, waiting for the bell to ring.

As usual, they are pushing each other, certainly not using their inside voices.

Alina drops out of formation and like a drill sergeant, barks commands.

"Okay, quiet."

"Stop pushing. I mean it."

The students are silent. They look at her.

Since they are used to her take-charge attitude, they obey.

They file in correctly.

After a few random comments, I announce I have a new seating chart since they must be tired of always sitting with the same people.

There is resistance as I direct students to their new seats.

Then they comply.

I am sure Alina is holding her breath, hoping I will not betray her as to who revised the seating chart.

It is amazing how well class goes with this new dynamic.

Alina continues to pressure and bully kids into better behavior.

"Knock it off. I can't hear," she tells them.

Alina, the saucy, pony-tailed, social director-turned-chief law enforcer of English class 5/4, has become my silent ally.

The Alina-effect lasts for a week or so: she can only do so much.

CHAPTER 59

The Administrative Visit Takes an Interesting Turn...

I FIND OUT, TO my delight, that two officials from my school district plan to visit me.

Sally Edwards and Jane Fulton decide to combine business with pleasure by paying me an administrative visit in France and sneaking in a bit of a French vacation.

Sally is the superintendent of schools, and Jane is a member of the school board.

Both are undoubtedly aware of the issues concerning Monique and her struggle teaching in the district. Ultimately, it was the joint decision of Sally and Susan, my principal, to let Monique remain teaching in our school.

Their officially stated objective is a courtesy visit.

Of course, they are not reluctant to take the opportunity to tour the Bordeaux region, and the vineyards of St Émilion, with us as their hosts.

On the first day of their visit, we drive to the city's center to explore the old town market, visit the cathedral, and dine in the *quartier* of Chartrons, known for its antique dealers.

The following day we wind our way along the left bank of the Gironde, through the world-renowned vineyards of *Château Mar-*

gaux, *Haut Médoc*, and *St Estèphe*; then double back to the right bank to *La Citadelle de Blaye*, a fortress built by Vauban for Louis XIV which has now fallen to ruins, gone its trappings of defense. We dine in the spectacular restaurant overlooking the estuary.

In our new role as tour guides, we discover we have come to feel enormous pride in our city and the outlying regions. Bordeaux herself has wooed us: we now consider ourselves *Bordelais*!

The official visit to the school is scheduled for a Friday. My friends attend the adorable 10:00 class and speak to the students. I am delighted the students understand the gist of their message in English. Fortunately, my visitors never see my rowdy English classes as they were not scheduled that day, or my reputation as an effective teacher would have taken a hit.

No visit would have been complete without a stopover in the faculty lounge.

I feel as proud to show them off as a camper on parents' week-end.

Several colleagues rise to the occasion to try their limited English.

Jeannette and Viviane chat with them at length.

We cross the courtyard during change of class, dodging the children who are playing a take-up game of soccer.

My English students cluster around us, shouting random sentences in English they have learned.

"It is a nice day today."

"I have three dogs."

"I like pizza."

"What is your name?"

Sally and Jane stop to respond to the students, which only produces giggles on the students' part.

We enter the administration building.

The secretaries, who are on high alert, rise to visit my guests.

The most senior escorts us to the principal's conference room.

The room is set up for formal entertainment.

Tidy white porcelain cups perched on saucers with doilies are lined up on a tray, along with an assortment of dry English tea cookies.

Monsieur Girard is at his wily best.

He seats them at the table with a bit of Gallic panache.

Madame Tabata, the head of discipline whom I have grown to admire, and Madame Colbert are gracious in their greeting. I serve as interpreter as the administrators exchange formalities.

Madame Colbert asks a few questions about their visit, as well as a few technical ones about the American school system.

During the visit, I realize how homesick I am for people I know.

Sally and Jane, although just friends, feel like my family. I will not be eager to see them leave.

They share the news that just before they left for France, our high school recently went through a bomb scare.

This has never happened before.

Someone called in a threat indicating there might be a device in the building. The police checked the premises thoroughly with dogs and found nothing.

School returns to normal but as an added security, the police return for several days with dogs to make a brief walk-through, to assure everyone all is well.

Monique, who does not like dogs for whatever reason, chooses to stay out of school the entire week, stating she is afraid and does not want to work in these conditions.

Our chat is interrupted by a phone call the principal takes. I think it must be important for the secretaries to interrupt this formal meeting.

The principal barely greets the caller. She turns her back to us as she listens to the caller for a few minutes. We can only hear someone speaking quickly.

Madame Colbert says, "Yes, yes, I understand your situation. I would not worry at all. This happens, even in France. No, you must not; you must return to work. No, I will not authorize that."

As my guests chat to serve as a distraction, I realize it is Monique on the phone. She is calling to get permission to stay out of school.

The timing of her call to Madame Colbert cannot be worse for her.

Madame Colbert passes the phone to me. Monique, searching for an ally, complains about what has happened. I tell her I am sorry, but there is nothing I can do.

It is the first time I have heard her voice since she screamed at me over the Christmas holidays.

Madame Colbert gives me a sign to end the conversation; she is embarrassed the American administrators are observing one of her staff being hysterical.

I can only imagine how Monique must have felt when she realized her American administrators were present while she was calling for permission to stay home until she felt comfortable returning to class.

I think to myself how timing is everything…

CHAPTER 60

Time Out for Good Behavior

WHILE MANY OF MY classes have become more manageable over the course of the school year, the English class 5/4 has not, because of the band of boys who are resistant to learning.

The good students in section 5/4 continue to be held hostage by them.

These unruly boys seem to be jealous of the ones who want to learn and try to divert attention away from the lesson by talking loudly, dropping books, making wisecracks, and exchanging silly looks. Anything they can do to disrupt the class.

It is everything I can do to stay the course.

If I can get a third of what I've planned done, I am pleased.

Monsieur Girard appears one day, unannounced and uninvited.

For fifteen minutes, he harangues the students, ranting at them about how lucky they are, and reminding them their only job as students is to take advantage of the native speaker who is their teacher.

Oh, they take advantage of me all right.

He paces up and down in front of the class. He reminds me of Perry Mason trying to convince the jury to acquit, only in a louder voice.

As I listen to him shout at the students, I wonder if this will be helpful or if he has actually undercut me and made this worse, since his presence implies I cannot manage on my own.

I weigh this for many days after.

Monsieur Girard leaves.

The class, a bit shell shocked, is quiet.

We continue on without interruption until the end of the hour.

Then a turn for the better.

Mireille, the teacher who decided to take a leave of absence in the fall and bequeathed me her wonderful 10:00 English class, returns to school.

For the rest of the year, she has been assigned library duty, and to my delight, assisting me in this 5/4 class on Mondays.

We decide if she can take the brigands into another classroom to work in a small group, for one hour a week I will be able to concentrate on teaching my motivated students. I will cram everything they need to know into this one precious hour a week.

We are hoping the band of boys might do better by themselves and learn better in a smaller setting where they can get individualized attention.

Ideally, it should be a win-win for all.

Mireille appears every Monday to summon her students.

They don't want to leave.

They resist.

They stay in their seats.

Mireille, who is no stranger to discipline, announces if they want to stay, they will also be assigned afterschool detention.

They leave.

I teach.

It is a precious time.

I deliver the concentrated lesson to the serious students, everything I want them to know for the week.

At the end of the hour, the other students return to class.

Their belligerence is palpable.

Mireille looks exhausted.

After class, she confesses she was not able to work with them.

They are like a pack of animals who bond together for destruction.

Mireille's frustration with them confirms for me that even native French teachers find it arduous to overcome negative behavior. All this time, I have been thinking it is just because I am not effective.

Mireille and I make a good team. We forge on *avec courage* to the end of the year.

May

CHAPTER 61

The Profession of Faith

AT THE CLOSE OF class on an ordinary day of an ordinary week in late May, René approaches my desk, lingering until his classmates have bolted out of the room.

"I have an invitation for you and Monsieur Donnelly," he says, dropping an envelope on my desk. He then leaves.

Inside is a hand-written invitation on yellow construction paper. On the cover is a hand-drawn smiling face encircled by glitter.

"I invite you to my profession of faith, which will take place Sunday, May 28th, at 10h30 a.m. at the church in St. Pierre, followed by a reception at our farm."

The address follows.

René has always been one of those students with whom I have a special connection.

At home, I ask, "What do you think, Patrick? Shall we go?"

We have no idea how many people are invited, and I wonder if Patrick will be all right surrounded by French speakers for the duration of the event.

Patrick's French is adequate; he understands everything said to him but hesitates to speak since he was never successful in studying it.

In college, his French professor agreed to give him a minimum passing grade, if he promised never to tell anyone who his French teacher was.

"We can always go and leave early if we want to," he replies.

We arrive at the church just before the ceremony and take our places in the back.

With the cue of the organ, René enters the church with his group, wearing a white robe. A wooden cross is hung around his neck on a white braided cord. His scuffed tennis shoes peek out under his angelic garb.

The Mass begins with the usual exhortation from the priest, several long-versed hymns, a sermon we could not hear very well, and the communion.

Proud parents and assorted family members snap photos as the children assemble in front of the altar to recite a rehearsed oath of divine allegiance to God and the Church.

At the end of the ceremony, the organ bellows the closing hymn as the young people process out behind the priest and his entourage.

The children, still in their white robes, accept kisses and embraces from the well-wishers of the congregation.

There is excited chatter as grandmothers stuff the program into their purses; family members and friends organize carpools, giving last-minute instructions as to where to meet for the reception.

We stand with René since we know no one.

We meet his parents who give us a map to their farm.

We follow the procession of little cars, vans, and a few trucks, out of town, to a narrow paved two-way road. On the left, down an embankment, we see the Garonne river, the same river which over-shot its banks during the hurricane and wiped out the small homes and farms on the lower side of the road.

René's family has a chicken and duck farm. The poultry is housed in long, narrow barns near the entry to their property.

Fortunately, before the hurricane, they had sold their stock for the holidays.

So many farmers were not that fortunate.

We leave the highway, turning off onto a cobblestone road.

The farmhouse, which is on our right, is classic fieldstone with a pitched roof. The mortar has compressed over time, but the build-ing is solid.

The house has been expanded on either side as the family grew.

We are to eat outside on long wooden tables in the garden across from the house. The table is bare but for a white plastic tablecloth secured by clothespins. Card table chairs, undoubtedly borrowed from a neighbor, line the long table.

René's father, seeing our parked car on the lawn, quickly comes out to greet us.

"Welcome, Monsieur and Madame Donnelly. René has so been looking forward to your joining us."

We chat a bit before he takes his leave to welcome other guests.

Wanting to snoop around a bit, I ask a friend of the family where I might wash my hands. The bathroom is in the main house, to the left of the large farm kitchen. The windows are small ovals set in the wall providing a little light to the shadowy room. There is a faint moldy smell of stone and time.

It strikes me that, in the kitchen, there is no sign of food being prepared.

Oh, we won't be staying long, I think.

The neighbors and extended family soon arrive and park on the lawn near our car.

Each person is carrying covered trays, or cartons, of food to the kitchen.

This is a good sign.

In a short time, the table is set; four wine glasses at each place predict *une grande fête.*

We are the stars of the event. The majority of invitees have never met an American and are intrigued René has an American English teacher.

A few French people speak halting English. We respond to their questions, answering slowly.

René has made place cards for each person. Our names are carefully written on yellow construction paper with the same design as the invitation.

Before dinner, René and his little sister, who, with her blond curly hair and smocked dress looks like a doll I had as a child, take us on a tour of the gardens.

There is a small vineyard, plus a vegetable garden of zucchini, tomatoes, and corn.

The apple orchard is set apart by a low wall made of irregular size stones held together by rough grey mortar.

René picks up his small brown dog in his arms and kisses it. I think how young and childlike he is, tender and vulnerable. What a responsibility I have as a teacher to nurture him in the hostile environment our school can be at times.

My place is to the right of his father, which touches me, as this is the place of honor.

Patrick is seated between two family friends who speak some English.

Our first course consists of trays of artisanal *foie gras*, made at René's home by his father, accompanied by a small glass of Sauternes.

The *foie gras* is smooth, creamy, and rich. We spread it on triangular toast, complemented by spicy farm-made cornichon pickles.

Next we are brought a soft Bibb lettuce salad marinated in a mild vinaigrette.

Trays of warm roast beef, pork, and chicken, fragrant gravy, golden crusty wedges of potatoes, small fingerling beans, follow and are served family-style, adding to the feeling of camaraderie among the guests.

The wine has been carefully selected to complement each course.

During the cheese course, René's father announces he is about to decant the bottles of wine he has reserved since the day René was born and saved for this occasion.

With drama, he opens the first bottle, closes his eyes as he sniffs the contents, and says, "Ah yes, this wine has aged well."

"Welcome, dear family and friends. We are so proud to have you with us to celebrate this wonderful day."

Santé!

The sun slants low through the branches in the late afternoon.

I look to Patrick, who is deep in a discussion of French history with his English-speaking table partner.

Chickens pass under the table. Ducks waddle nearby.

The afternoon is so dreamlike, it is like being in a pastoral French movie.

Mellowed by the company and the wines, we reluctantly arise to leave.

What seemed like a task, responding to the invitation of a young student, becomes one of the loveliest afternoons of our life.

June

CHAPTER 62

The Agony and The Ecstasy

SUMMER COMES TO BORDEAUX suddenly.

The students awaken from the humdrum stupor of winter feeling frisky and decidedly unmanageable.

The classroom, with little ventilation from the windows, is oven-hot.

It is early June. The school year will end soon. This stretch of weeks is stressful for even the most seasoned French teacher.

Arriving at school on the first Monday of the month, I read in the announcements the fatal dictum that the grades will be due the following week. Equally deadly, the librarian requires all books to be collected soon so she can do her tidy inventory of worn covers, broken bindings, and lost books.

This is dreadful news.

One of the greatest powers and protections a teacher has is that of the impending grade. Without this menace and without textbooks, I cannot imagine how I will manage the students.

But this is the French system, and I must abide by it.

Now I must make copies of lessons from the MIA textbooks, require the students to do homework pages, and hope for the best. They know, and I know, this is a waste of time.

"Oh, I'm sorry. I left my work at home."

"Did you give us work on Friday?"

"I lost my paper; do you have another?"

The balance of the school year feels like I am in the waiting room of an airport and my plane is endlessly and hopelessly delayed.

Of course, I say nothing to my colleagues, but interiorly, I am screaming, "This is insane."

The last week, I weaken and show the movie *Shakespeare in Love*, subtitled in French, under the flimsy guise of a cultural benefit. No one is fooled, but it does pass the time, and they love it.

At noon, during this untenable period, I have one of the most touching experiences of my life.

I go to the faculty room. There all of the teachers are assembled. There is a bright linen tablecloth on three rectangular tables pushed together. *Foie gras*, red wine, champagne, salads, bread, meat trays, and condiments are set out. Yellow, green, and blue crepe paper streamers are looped gaily, taped to the ceiling.

I blurt, "Is this the party for the end of the school year? I thought that was next week?"

"No, Jackie, this is for you!"

Laurence leads me by the hand to the front of the room. The faculty applauds and cheers.

"Bravo, Jackie."

I am given a collective gift of an Hermès scarf featuring the monuments of Paris, and a commemorative book with each teacher's sentimental remarks about me. Best of all, Laurence has written a poem in alexandrine verse, a pastiche of my favorite writer, Corneille, lyrically expressing the affection the faculty and staff have for me.

"Oh rage, oh despair, oh vacation, our enemy
Must we see leave, our dear friend, Jackie...."

I look at the warm faces that have been my support throughout the year, so delighted to express their affection for me.

We have been together in the trenches for this long, demanding year; our bond is now deeply rooted in my heart.

This moment confirms what I have grown to understand.

The French are not smilers or glad handers.

They take their time getting to know you.

However, as in *Le Petit Prince*, their friendship evolves bit by bit; as the fox instructs *le petit prince* in Saint-Exupéry's story, the French must be "tamed".

But once they are your friends, they are forever there for you.

This is borne out by Louise and Paul coming to my immediate rescue at Christmas with the tree; and how Bruno, Laurence, Jeannette, Mireille, and Viviane supported me all through the year. By the camaraderie at the *vendanges chez* Remy, the spectacular meal in René's family home, and the affection of our neighbors Diane and Alex, their door always open to us.

And how, here in this simple faculty workroom, where I spent so much time with my colleagues, I am *fêted* in such an authentic, heartfelt way. I am touched beyond measure.

CHAPTER 63

The End Times

In June, the school schedule offers a bit of diversion.

My English class 5/4 is scheduled for a field trip to Bordeaux on a Friday to see an exhibition of mockups of aircrafts in one of the hangars along the quay.

If you visit Bordeaux today, this area has been renovated, taking advantage of the gorgeous views from the river.

At the time, however, there was a series of storage buildings marred by graffiti.

Patrick and I intend to spend the weekend in the Dordogne, so we decide this exhibit would be fun to see, and Laurence, who organized the day, could benefit from extra chaperones.

I take the bus with the students, while Patrick follows behind in our car.

I sit in the back with Alina and her chums. Some of the more problematic boys from the class are seated nearby, which gives me a chance to chat with them.

I realize they really are lovely kids outside of the classroom.

When I ask them about their lives, what they like to do, and what they like to eat, they open up and are very chatty.

Here at the end of the year, on this bus, we have made a truce; we have a moment when our guards are down, and we can enjoy being together.

Alina decides to lead us in a few songs to pass the time.

The guide greets our group at the door and leads us to the first exhibit, that of the Concorde, the British-French supersonic plane which at the time was still in operation.

The questions some of my students ask are so basic, I realize how little intellectual nourishment they have at home. At one point, the guide is impatient with them, thinking they are mocking her by their naïve comments.

We pass from exhibit to exhibit, the kids fascinated by the displays. It is touching to see their enthusiasm.

At noon, we sit on the low stone wall near the river to eat our bag lunches, teachers and students feeling at one with each other.

It is a good break from classes.

As the end of the school year approaches, teachers and students see the end in sight.

There is a palpable euphoria we all feel during the last week of school.

But this year, it is a time of unexpected nostalgia for me, as I prepare to say goodbye to my colleagues and students.

I believe this mixed feeling of elation and sadness is shared by many of my students.

In my locker, I find multiple bottles of wine the students have brought to school with kind notes from their parents.

I can't imagine bottles of wine safely arriving at school in the States.

The parents of a visually impaired girl in one of my eighth-grade classes, whom I helped all year by submitting quizzes and tests in advance so they could be transcribed into Braille, offer me a large decorative box of brandy with two snifters.

My colleagues watch with wonder when I show them the gifts.

To their delight, I give most of the wine away since I will be taking a plane back to Paris, and I do not have room in my suitcase for all the bottles.

Two students have conspired to make a tape of their favorite songs interspersing affectionate messages to me in English.

I receive handmade greeting cards signed by classes of students.

But nothing can measure up to the last class meeting of my memorable 5/4.

When I arrive in class, I can see through the door the students are already in their seats.

This is alarmingly unusual.

Alina blocks my entry into the classroom.

"*Un, deux, trois,*" she counts, before allowing me to enter. I am stunned to see them in party mode. René, the student representative, offers me a large bouquet of flowers.

Alina takes my hand and seats me in front of the class.

The students, under the baton of Alina stand to sing a poem they have written to the melody of "I Will Survive," albeit in French, not English.

Oh, Madame Donnelly
You are so wonderful
Do not leave us, we ask, no, don't leave us...

How did they know that of all the songs they could have chosen, "I Will Survive" was my theme song for the year, the one I used to hum from the beginning of the year?

There is a large cake, mounds of cookies, and little gifts which I open with tears in my eyes.

A few chide me with anecdotes from the year.

One of the boys says, "Ah, you were so funny when you got mad at us."

"Remember when we hid your bell?"

"We love the game we played. What was it called?"

Many speak in English, sometimes parroting a dialogue from that stuffy book.

We spend the hour laughing, reminiscing and celebrating the end of our time together.

I stand up to help clean the dishes.

Alina says, "Sit down, please, Madame. This is your party; you are not to work."

The students, like busy bees, straighten up the room.

The final bell rings. I stand at the door, saying goodbye to each one. These students, as well as the others, are lovely kids.

I will miss them.

If I only had known the heroine would succeed in the final reel, my year would have been much easier.

CHAPTER 64

Ce n'est qu'un Au Revoir

AN AUDIBLE YELP IS heard when the last afternoon bell rings. The students are released and are on vacation. Like a herd of cattle breaking through the fence, their thunderous footsteps resound as they run down the stairs and out the door to the sun and summer.

It is over.

Patrick returned to the States a few days ago.

I spend my final Saturday packing.

Saturday night, I dine with Louise and Paul at the golf club. Madame Saule, who did not remember my name in the fall, now hugs me like a family member.

"Dessert is on the house. And why not a few glasses of champagne?" she offers.

Sunday is my final neighbor dinner with Diane and Alex.

I walk around the fence to their home for the last time.

We reminisce about this year, my wild hair color, the excursions we took together, the fast pop-in visits, and the many shared meals.

Their friendship has been my anchor; the affectionate bond we forged as neighbors and friends seasoned my time in Bordeaux with joy.

We dawdle over coffee, not wanting the evening to end.

The following Monday is a teacher workday, cleaning the classroom, turning in last reports, and tying up loose ends.

After a long and challenging school term, I feel a sudden nostalgia for this school and certainly for my colleagues; I somewhat, almost, wish I could stay on for another year.

I imagine I would do so much better the second time around since now I know the ropes.

Instead, I will return to Paris to decompress for a weekend with Joëlle before going home.

The release from my responsibilities I so longed for all year, now makes me wistful.

I go to my classroom to work and muse. The windows are closed.

I open the first window near my desk and sit down.

It is quiet.

I lean back in my chair and review the year as if I am watching a movie. I picture the many scenes that took place in my classroom.

I see my 10:00 *chouchou* class arriving enthusiastically and affectionately. So easy to teach. So delightful to be with.

The scene changes to my more challenging students and their antics. There I am, standing at the desk, my fingers clenched as I make my way through the lesson.

Every corner of the classroom evokes memories.

In this classroom I have succeeded, and I have failed.

I have tried to do well.

There is a nagging question I have mulled over in my mind from the onset of this adventure.

Knowing what I know now, would I have left the comfortable, safe and sure life I had in the States to go through the highs and lows of this experience?

Would I have been content to turn down this opportunity or always regret not having dared to do it?

The answer comes from my heart.

I would choose to repeat every moment of this school year, no matter how tough it proved to be. Every experience has only served to make me stronger.

This exchange has fulfilled my dreams to accept the ultimate personal and professional challenge: to live as the French live and function as they do in their culture.

Of course, France offers a myriad of wonders. Visits to the romantic castles of the Loire valley, tastings of regional wines paired perfectly with gourmet meals, the delight of wading in the vivid blue Mediterranean near the sandy beaches of Cannes and riding up to the peaked mountains of Chamonix. And... Paris. Paris, Paris!

But as my friend Nicole says, "France is a garden only for tourists." Meaning that beneath the romantic veneer is a country like all others, with day-to-day problems not apparent to the tourist.

Having spent a year in France, I am a little less rosy-eyed about French society having seen her underpinnings.

Now, France, to me, seems like a piece of embroidery.

As a student, a teacher, and a frequent visitor, I had only seen the lovely side, the gardens, the flowers, the romance of it all.

Living in France has allowed me to turn over the fabric to see the reverse side where the knots and the broken thread are hidden.

Thanks to this year in Bordeaux I can also turn the embroidery right side over again, to look at the pattern with more appreciation and understanding than I had before. France with all of her foibles still captivates me.

She has become an intimate part of me and I of her.

For this reason, I would not give up this experience for anything; for through this baptism of fire, I now appreciate France in a deeper dimension.

I do think my biggest surprise this year is that teaching in France has been so much harder than I could have imagined when I sat with Patrick on our screened-in porch looking over the lake, on that lovely evening when we decided to leave it all and run away.

I knew – or assumed - teaching in another country might be a challenge. But St. Pierre raised the stakes even higher, as this was a year of organizational conflict, strikes, and teaching rebellious students, many of whom needed special professional attention I could not offer.

What I have learned, above all, is I am stronger than I thought I was.

When my back was to the wall in early September, realizing the extent of the task to which I feel incapable, I drew on an inner strength to survive I did not know was in me.

When I thought I would crack or run: I didn't.

I will treasure the school calendar I kept on my desk at the house, onto which, even before removing my coat, I marked off another day, somewhat like a prisoner making marks on the rough stone wall of his cell.

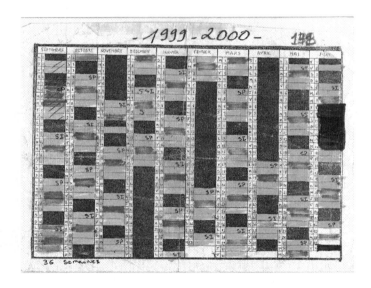

Now, I rise to put the English textbooks away in the locker, along with Monique's notebooks and classroom supplies.

With a Kleenex, I affectionately dust off my desk for the last time.

I go to the window and look out at the courtyard.

Today it is empty, and I picture my students, home now, enjoying their summer days. I will not see them when they return in the fall.

I am alone with my thoughts.

But not really.

There is a presence.

I turn to the door to see Alina and René, who have been watching me.

"What are you doing here, my dears? You should be far from school; you are free."

They approach my desk.

In Alina's hand is a card they bought and signed. "To my wonderful teacher."

Alina says, "I will miss you, Madame. I am sorry for giving you a difficult time in class. You really did teach us well. "

René, much shyer, simply nods his head.

"I promise to keep studying. I learned a lot this year," he adds.

I am so touched they have returned for a last goodbye!

We chat for a bit, but really everything has been said.

"Walk me downstairs, please," I ask.

It is time to close the classroom.

With one last click of the key, I leave.

I will not return.

With hugs and warm wishes, they leave me at the faculty lounge door.

I walk in the lounge to see Jeannette, Mireille, Laurence, and Bruno chatting over coffee. "This is goodbye," I say.

They rise to give me hugs.

"Jackie, are you sure you don't want to stay?" It is tempting as I feel such a part of this faculty: it is wrenching to leave.

We, as colleagues, have been through a lot.

There were two more short strikes in the spring after the first one that felled Madame Laubert. Laurence, my dear friend, got me through them all with her counsel and support.

I worked with or around Monsieur Girard, as my colleagues did.

I thrived under the new principal, Madame Colbert; it is hard saying goodbye to her.

And I truly care for my students.

But I have to go.

My plane for Paris is in three hours.

I must leave because Monique is scheduled to return today. Sadly, I do not want to see her again.

I am disappointed our relationship fell apart.

I will always wonder who she is.

I hope she thinks back on her year in the States as fondly as I do my year in France. I trust she will.

I also imagine her family, who will be delighted to be home again, will be pleased with the tidy house, and see that despite my Christmas tree pyre fiasco, we have taken good care of their home.

So, it is time.

Final, lingering hugs. I leave the lounge.

Crossing the courtyard for the last time, I hear the strains of "Auld Lang Syne" as Jeannette, Mireille, Bruno, and Laurence sing over the microphone in the office:

Ce n'est qu'un au revoir, Jackie

Ce n'est qu'un au revoir.

It is only until we see each other again, Jackie,

It is only until we see each other again!

I look back and wave at them, blowing kisses.

I look up at the dark windows of my classroom with a deep sense of personal satisfaction and affection.

This is it.

I did it.

I survived.

I head for the gate, and pausing, turn back for one last look.

Acknowledgments

To my stalwart, patient, and talented editor, Judyth Hill, whose support and enthusiasm for the project matched her top-notch professional work. Judyth was editor, cheerleader, critic, and friend through this writing process.

To the talented Mary Meade, who designed the cover and book interior.

To Alice Neufeld, who was my Beta reader and offered great insight and suggestions. Alice ended up memorizing the book.

To Carole Schor, my proofreader, who gave the fine and final polish.

To Anna Knutson Geller, a publishing agent, who gave excellent advice.

To Laurence Mokrani, my dear colleague and amie, who supported me through this year in France.

To Joëlle CC who is my lifelong sounding board and interpreter of all things French.

To my colleagues at "St. Pierre," friends and mentors, who taught me so much about living and teaching in France. I admire you so.

And to Mrs. Coghlan, a family friend, who, when I was eight, predicted I would become a writer.